Schoolteacher and Saint

A
Biography
of

Saint Lucy Filippini

PASCAL P. PARENTE, S.T.D., PH.D.

ILLUSTRATED BY PAUL A. GROUT

Grail Publication

St. Meinrad   Indiana

NIHIL OBSTAT:
JOSEPH G. KEMPF, PH.D.
Censor librorum

IMPRIMATUR:
✠ PAUL C. SCHULTE, D.D.
Archbishop of Indianapolis

December 17, 1953

Library of Congress Catalog Card Number 54-11552

INTRODUCTION

The brief allocution given by Pope Pius XI, on March 21, 1926, on the occasion of the approval of the three miracles needed for the Beatification of Lucy Filippini, offers an appropriate introduction to the present biography.

"Lucy Filippini, the Saintly Teacher"—said the Pontiff—"model and molder of saintly teachers, was marvelously suited to her own times and to the time in which Divine Providence, recalling her memory through the glory of miracles, has once more proposed her example to our imitation.

"A Saintly Teacher, the spiritual mother of saintly teachers, at the turn of the seventeenth century and beginning of the eighteenth—a period of so much ignorance and so much moral decadence in spite of the faith and the exterior form of Christian life—Lucy Filippini devoted herself to a wonderful sort of apostolate. Having first been an apostle of her own sanctification, she, with the cooperation of her loyal associates, became the apostle of so many souls, so many families, in such a wide social circle.

"Now, after such a long lapse of time, she still remains the Saintly Teacher, the Foundress of saintly teachers. She is once more brought into the foreground, today, in order that all may see and imitate her, at a time when the need for the sanctification of the teaching profession is greater than ever, when the school has become almost everything—the beginning of everything, the essence of everything. This is a time when it is more than ever necessary for the school to become the beginning of truth and of Christian education,the vestibule of the great temple of the Church."[1]

The sanctification of the teaching profession, demanded here by the Pope, cannot be attained except by personal spiritual endeavor, with every teacher, religious or lay, seriously and constantly striving after Christian perfection. The sanctification of the teachers will bring about a sanctification of the school and prepare a new generation of men and women, inspired not only by the word but also by the example of their teachers.

School teaching is more than an ordinary career or profession, it is a vocation. For St. Lucy Filippini school teaching was an apostolate, a true Catholic action. Only saintly teachers will be ever able to make a school, "the vestibule of the great temple of the Church." Our present generation more than any other has realized the great truth contained in Tommaseo's words: When a school ceases to be a temple, it becomes a den.

Schoolteacher and Saint is the first original work in English on St. Lucy Filippini. A look at the list of our sources shows that except for a few Latin documents all the sources are Italian. Whatever translation of these sources appears in this book is our own.

We express our gratitude to the Religious Teachers Filippini of Villa Walsh, Morristown, N. J., and of Villa Victoria Academy, Trenton, N. J. for having suggested the writing of this book and for the many ways they helped us, with valuable information, by placing at our disposal many important documents, and by supplying us with all the pictures published in this book. We trust that the present work in promoting the cause of their Foundress, St. Lucy Filippini, will also contribute in promoting their own.   *The Author*

[1] SALOTTI, Card. Carlo. *La Santa Lucia Filippini.* Pag. 341.

CONTENTS

ST. LUCY FILIPPINI
Foundress of the Religious Teachers Filippini

CHAPTER ONE

A LIFE THAT ENDS IN GLORY.

THE Angelus bell was ringing in the campanile of the old Cathedral in the town of Montefiascone, on Lake Bolsena, on March 25, 1732, when the *Maestra Santa*—the Saintly Teacher —breathed her last.

It was the noon hour of the day on which the Church commemorates the announcement of the Incarnation by the Angel Gabriel to the Virgin Mary. The departed had always hoped to die on a Feast of the Madonna. Her pious wish has been fulfilled—on Our Lady Day she passed from this life with a smile on her lips. On this day the Son of God had come down to dwell among men, and she—the Saintly Teacher—left the earth to live with the Angels forever.

Her remains were buried under the floor of Our Lady's Chapel in the Cathedral Church. A wreath of flowers—symbol of her virginity—was placed on her brow, and a few fresh and fragrant hyacinths—sweet harbingers of spring—were laid at her feet in the casket together with a metal tube enclosing a Latin parchment which said in part:

"Here rests the body of LUCY FILIPPINI, a woman of outstanding piety.... Asleep bodily in deep slumber when the

1

Lord came but with her heart awake and ready for the heavenly nuptials."[1]

As the heavy stone fell like a trap door upon the subterranean vault some may have thought perhaps that the pall of oblivion had fallen upon a beautiful life.

While her mortal remains sleep there in the darkness of the tomb, her virginal soul, unstained and pure as a lily or mountain snow, is enshrined in the glory of Heaven. Her religious foundations continue unabated on earth and her example of Christian virtue continues with undiminished splendor to guide thousands of her spiritual daughters. On such a life, the pall of oblivion could never fall. In Lucy Filippini the words of the Scripture were fulfilled: "O how beautiful is the chaste generation with glory, for the memory thereof is immortal: because it is known both with God and with men. When it is present, they imitate it; and they desire it when it hath withdrawn itself, and it triumpheth crowned forever, winning the reward of undefiled conflicts."[2] The memory of the Saints never dies because they are God's friends and God glorifies the name of those who have honored Him on earth.

Virtue itself—especially when heroic and persevering— breeds immortality. "Virtue makes men on the earth famous" —said Chilo, one of the Seven Wise Men—"in their grave illustrious, in the heaven immortal." All this has now happened to Lucy, whose life like her name was light and music.

One hundred twenty-six years passed after Lucy's burial before there was any thought of opening her grave. At the for-

[1] *Hic iacet corpus Luciae Filippini insignis pietatis faeminae . . . Corpore sopitam gravi lethargo, se corde vigilantem, paratamque ad caelestes nuptias invenit Dominus.* P. BERGAMASCHI. *Vita della Ven. Lucia Filippini.* Vol. II, pag. 266.
[2] Wisd. 4:1 f.

mal request of Sister Margherita Balducci, Superior of the Religious Teachers Filippini of Montefiascone, the grave was officially opened in the presence of the local Ordinary, Bishop Jona, his Pro-Vicar General, his Chancellor, three lay witnesses, and a large number of Religious Teachers both from Montefiascone and from Rome on April 24, 1858.

They found the casket well preserved and in perfect condition. It was lifted up from the vault and opened in the presence of the above mentioned authorities and witnesses. The bridal wreath was still there on her brow—symbol of her virginity. There was nothing exceptional in this because the flowers were artificial, but the lily-like perfume, diffused from the open coffin of one who had died of cancer, caused no less a sensation than the almost complete preservation of her body. The admiration of the authorities and the witnesses grew exceedingly when the hyacinths of the hundred and twenty-six springtimes past were found at her feet, still fresh and fragrant as the day they were placed there. A number of witnesses who deposed in the process of Beatification mentioned this circumstance of the fresh flowers.

"As the coffin was opened some hyacinths were found in it, as fresh and as fragrant as if just picked. This fact made a deeper impression on the witness than all the other particulars."[3]

This circumstance appears even more extraordinary when we read further in the document of recognition of the remains that most of her outer garments had decomposed and had to be replaced with new ones. The Latin parchment found in the casket was read. The old document gave ample evidence of the outstanding piety and heroic virtue of Lucy Filippini to a new

[3] *Faliscodunensis, Beatificationis et Canonizationis Servae Dei Luciae Filippini.* Summarium, Num. XVI, 111.

generation of her spiritual daughters who now looked for the first time upon those loved features of their mother and teacher. Yet the sweet language of those flowers that had never lost their freshness and their fragrance was more eloquent to them than the Latin classical document in transmitting to a distant generation in their own language the odor of sanctity of God's servant.

Her body having been clothed afresh was enclosed in a double casket and buried in front of the altar of Our Lady in the same Cathedral.

The unforgettable example of virtue and good works and the many miraculous cures obtained from God through her intercession from the day of her funeral impelled her spiritual daughters to start formal canonical procedure leading to Lucy's Canonization. She herself seems to have taken the first step in that direction.

One day towards the end of August of the year 1903, a young Sister, Mary Donati, of the Motherhouse of Montefiascone, who was working for a teacher's diploma, became dangerously sick of typhus fever. Despairing of her life, the Community as always interceded with their saintly Foundress, Lucy Filippini, for the recovery of the sick Sister. A picture of the Foundress was kept near the bed of Sister Donati. The attending Sister had just left the sick room in order to join the Community at supper one evening, when Lucy Filippini entered the sick room.

"My daughter, you will not die of this infirmity. You will not be able to receive your diploma this year, but you will receive it later."

"Oh, Mother, give us some of your spirit!"—pleaded Sister Donati.

"Do all things for the glory of God!"—replied the Foundress. Then, she herself made a request.

"Tell the Superior to work for my Beatification."

"But, Mother, how can we do that?—It costs so much money!"

"The Holy Father will take care of the expense."

Sister Donati eventually recovered, she obtained her diploma a year later, and for many years she taught in the schools of Montefiascone. She is still living and in good health as we are writing this.

When St. Lucy said that the Holy Father would take care of the expense involved in the long process of Beatification and Canonization, she was simply calling attention to the unique nature of her foundation, the *Maestre Pie Filippini*—Religious Teachers Filippini. This is a Pontifical Institute, not in the ordinary canonical sense given to religious congregations that have received the final approbation of the Holy See, but in a very specific manner determined by the Apostolic Letter of Pope Leo XII, dated October 6, 1828. In virtue of this Papal document the Religious Teachers Filippini are immediately subject to the Holy Father, and are placed under the jurisdiction of the Apostolic Almoner who governs the Institute—both in spiritual and economic matters—with ordinary jurisdiction in the name of the Pontiff himself.

The latest edition of the Rule of the Institute, which was personally examined, approved, and signed by His Holiness Pope Pius XII, has the following article:

"The Institute is governed with ordinary jurisdiction by His Excellency the Secret Almoner of His Holiness, according to the Apostolic Letter *Praeter Puerorum Institutionem* of Leo XII, October 6, 1828, and the Decree of the Sacred Congrega-

tion of Bishops and Regulars of March 21, 1896. Therefore, the
houses of this Institute, no matter where they may be located,
are exempt from the jurisdiction of the local Ordinary, except in
cases expressly mentioned in the Code of Canon Law."[4]

By experience acquired here on earth, Lucy knew that the
Holy See would take care of her needs now as it had from the
day she opened her first school in Rome in May, 1707. In the
light of glory, she saw the will of God in her regard and the
manner in which the divine will would be carried out.

Divine Providence seems to have waited so long for the glorification of Lucy Filippini here on earth because it wanted to fo-
cus the light of her virtuous life upon our modern generation.
Her apostolate of Catholic Action, her form of Religious Communities following evangelical perfection without religious
vows and dedicated exclusively to the apostolate of teaching are
more imperative today than they were in her own generation.
She was two hundred years ahead of her time.

It was reserved to the saintly Pontiff Blessed Pius X to sign
the decree for the introduction of the cause of her Beatification
and Canonization on July 10, 1912. On November 25, 1924,
Pope Pius XI solemnly declared the virtue of Lucy Filippini
as heroic, and, on March 21, 1926, the same Pontiff issued the
decree approving three miracles obtained from God at the
intercession of Lucy Filippini.

The two essential conditions—heroic virtue and miracles—
having been happily fulfilled, the way was open for the solemn
ceremony of her Beatification in the largest Church of Christen-
dom, the Basilica of St. Peter in Vatican City.

The joy and happiness of the Religious Teachers Filippini

[4] *Regole del Pontificio Istituto delle Maestre Pie Filippini.* Art. 129.

seemed a reflection of the heavenly bliss and glory of their spiritual mother when on June 13, 1926, they assisted at her Beatification. The decree of Beatification having been read, a veil fell from the so-called Gloria of Bernini in the Basilica of St. Peter, revealing the triumphant picture of Blessed Lucy Filippini. In the same instant the sudden flash of thousands of lights, the music of the organ and of the thousands of voices singing the *Te Deum* turned the Basilica of St. Peter into a vision of Heaven. It is an experience that has no equal on earth. Tears of joy prevented many of the Sisters present from joining in the liturgical hymn of thanksgiving, their eyes fixed on that picture of Blessed Lucy in the light and glory that no passing cloud shall darken again. They thought of the zeal, the many bitter trials, the hardships of one who had been an orphan, a teacher, an apostle! . . . They recalled the words of the Scripture: "They that instruct many to justice shall shine as stars for all eternity."[5]

The joy of that memorable day was to be enhanced by another extraordinary event. At the very moment of the Beatification in St. Peter's Basilica, Sister Nicolina Gennari of the Religious Teachers of Rome was miraculously cured of a long standing ulcerous tuberculosis of the lungs by intercession of Blessed Lucy. Before a month had passed, on June 6 of that same year, a boy, Anthony Manieri, was suddenly and completely cured of bronchopneumonia by the same intercession. On May 11, 1930, the Holy See officially approved these two new miracles and, seven days later declared that the Canonization of Blessed Lucy Filippini could now take place.

Thus with solemn Canonization on June 22, 1930, she who by popular acclamation had been called the Saintly Teacher

[5] Dan. 12:3.

became officially a Saint of the Church of God. This was the third and final step into that glory that cannot be made void, the glory, the peace, and the joy that God gives and the world cannot take away.

Those who looked at St. Lucy Filippini in the glory of her Canonization could hardly think of her as of one who had died. It seemed like a resurrection, a victory over sin, over death, a real glorification. Even that silent tomb in the Cathedral of Montefiascone reflected all the glory and the joy of that day of triumph. Every Christian believes that the mortal remains enclosed therein will one day be resumed and be transformed by the immortal spirit of a Saint, a virgin spouse of Christ, to follow the Lamb, for timeless ages, singing that canticle that only virgin souls can sing.

There is no fairer appraisal of a man's life than the one made at his death and judgment. For this reason the Apostles of Christ began their preaching from the death and resurrection of their Master. The rest of the Gospel came later, and was easily understood once the shame of the Cross and the glory of the Resurrection were accepted.

We have followed this method in presenting the life of one of Christ's faithful servants, St. Lucy Filippini, telling first of her death and glorification.

The disciples of the Divine Master were still crushed under the heavy burden of the cross, which had seemed to have fallen on all of them too when it was placed on the shoulders of their Master.

"Why so sad?"—asked the risen Savior, on Easter Sunday, of two of them on the way to Emmaus. "Did not the Christ have to suffer these things before entering into his glory?"[6] The way

6 Luke, 24:17-26.

of the cross was the way to that glory, from the manger of Bethlehem to the cross of Calvary. The way to glory for Lucy Filippini was no different. An unseen cross was left in her cradle the first year of her life when her mother died. For sixty long years she carried that cross as the following life story will tell.

CHAPTER TWO

LIFE BEGINS WITH TEARS.

SOME thirty-five miles northwest of Rome on the shores of the Tyrrhenian sea, there is a very ancient town, Tarquinia that gave old Rome two of its kings: Tarquin the Elder, and Tarquin the Proud.

Tarquin the Elder, drained the Forum and enclosed it with porticos, enlarged what was later known as the Circus Maximus, and built the Cloaca Maxima. This latter subterranean structure, paralleling the Pyramids in extent and massiveness, far surpasses them in the difficulty of execution. It is so gigantic that the more one examines it, the more inconceivable it seems that even a large and powerful state could have constructed it. It consists of semicircles whose immense square blocks, without mortar, have not moved a knife's thickness since the day they were placed nearly three thousand years ago. This gigantic structure has been the main drain and sewer system for both pagan and Christian Rome, and even today Tarquin's monumental work serves admirably in keeping streets and parks dry and clean in the City of the Seven Hills.

The surname, Proud, is comment enough for the other Tarquin. His arrogance and the crimes of his children brought the royal system of government in the city of Rome to an end.[1]

The site of the ancient Etruscan town of Tarquinia is just outside the present city. Its few remaining ruins give evidence of a great power and a great civilization, especially in the well preserved hypogea—subterranean burial places—whose paintings date back many centuries before the Christian era. Tarquinia—the Etruscan *Tarchuna,* Greek: ΤΑΡΚΥΝΙΑ— was the ancient capital of one of the most powerful states of the Etruscan confederation, extending from the Thyrrhenian sea to Lake Bolsena. Recent archeological finds prove conclusively that there was a civilized center on this site as early as the beginning of the first millennium before Christ.[2]

The present town of Tarquinia had about 2300 inhabitants at the time of our story; it has about 9000 today. It looks like a fortress with its towers, city-walls, and battlements, rising on a rocky spur, on the left bank of the river Marta, some five hundred feet above sea level. It offers an enchanting view of the blue sea with the little islands of Giglio, Montecristo, and Giannutri on one side, and of cultivated fields, hills, and mountains on the other. During the early Middle Ages the population of Tarquinia, extremely reduced in number, took refuge in the near-by town of Corneto situated on top of a hill. The merging of the two towns gave origin to the double name Corneto Tarquinia which was prevalent during the whole period of our story. By a royal decree, issued April 23, 1922, the name Corneto was officially abolished and the old historical name of Tarquinia was applied to the whole zone.

Here Lucy—the flower and pride of all the maids of ancient

[1] C. MERIVALE. *History of Rome.* Pag. 21.
[2] *Enciclopedia Italiana,* at the word *Tarquinia.*

and modern Tarquinia—was born on January 13, 1672 . She was the fifth and last child of Philip Filippini and Magdalen Picchi, a well-to-do, devout couple, who ranked among the first families of the town.

The infant was baptized the same day in the local Cathedral church by her paternal uncle, the Reverend Michael Filippini, both Canon and Rector of the Cathedral.

At Baptism the infant was named LUCIA. No better name could be given to a little girl who was to become a religious teacher, an apostle, a Saint.

Looking into the sleepy eyes of his tiny, little niece, Canon Michael Filippini asked:

"Lucy, what dost thou ask of the Church of God?"

"Faith," replied her sponsor.

"What doth Faith bring thee to?"

"Life everlasting," said the sponsor in Lucy's name. After this answer, the infant received her first lesson in spiritual perfection.

"If, therefore," continued her uncle, "thou will enter into life, keep the commandments. Thou shalt love the Lord thy God with all thy heart, and with all thy soul, and with all thy mind, and thy neighbor as thyself."

The inspiring ceremony continued till she was born again in the waters of Baptism, becoming a new creature, an adopted daughter of God, an heir to the kingdom of Heaven, a member of the Mystical Body of Christ. Through sanctifying grace she had become a temple of the Holy Spirit, a mansion of the Blessed Trinity. The Church gave her the white robe which every guest must wear at the banquet of the King of Heaven.

"Receive this white garment"—said the officiating uncle, putting all his soul in these words—"which mayest thou carry without stain before the judgment seat of our Lord Jesus Christ, that thou mayest have life everlasting."

The ceremony was almost over, just one more symbol and then the final blessing. The symbol assumed a particular meaning in this case. A light was given to Lucy whose name means light. It was the lamp the prudent virgin, Lucy, would keep always burning, waiting for the coming of the heavenly Bridegroom.

"Receive this burning light, and keep thy baptism so as to be without blame: observe the commandments of God, that when our Lord shall come to His nuptials, thou mayest meet Him together with all the saints in the heavenly court, and live for ever and ever."[3]

"Amen," answered her sponsor and Lucy's Guardian Angel. The deep meaning of this ceremony is fully realized when we compare it with the other ceremony that took place on June 13, 1926, two hundred fifty-four years later, in the basilica of St. Peter in Rome, when that same Lucy Filippini was beatified and was seen in the glory of the Saints. The seed of sanctity and of eternal life implanted in her soul at Baptism had reached its full development on earth and found its eternal reward in the glory of Heaven. This the Church really expects of all her children, because all those who are baptized in the Lord Jesus are called to be saints.

Little Lucy was brought home to her mother who received her with reverence and inexplicable joy, as if she were an Angel of God.

The first day of her life on earth came to an end, a day that had brought her the greatest gifts, that of life and that of Grace,

[3] Roman Ritual. The Baptism of Infants.

as a child of her parents and a child of God. There was good reason for thanking God that evening, but little Lucy was sleeping and her Angel had to do all the thanking and praising for her. One day she herself would thank God with her whole heart and soul for those gifts.

The cold winter days were soon over, and when the long balmy days of spring, full of sunshine and flowers, reached the Tarquinian shores, little Lucy began to distinguish colors and faces about her. There was one face which was like sunshine itself. The smile and love of those eyes told her this was her mother, she was so good to her. It is thus that children begin to learn. Their knowledge is based mostly on love like that of mystic souls.

"Begin, O little child to recognize thy mother by her smile."[4]

Lucy was only eleven months old when that smiling face disappeared. On December 22, 1672, death took little Lucy's mother. She died in the prime of life, at the age of twenty-seven. That day the cross—unseen—entered Lucy's life never to leave it again.

Philip Filippini concentrated all his care and affection on the three children left him by their mother. The children were John Francis, seven years old, Elizabeth who was about four, and the little infant Lucy. The Filippinis had two other children who presumably died in their infancy, for their names never appear in connection with Lucy's life as narrated by her earliest biographer. Little Lucy received most of her father's attention and affection. In this he was followed closely by his brother, Canon Michael, who had baptized the little girl and who was now asking another Mother, the Blessed Virgin Mary, to take the

---

[4] VIRGIL. *Incipe, parve puer, risu cognoscere matrem.* Buc. IV, 60.

Lucy Builds Little Altars

15

place of his deceased sister-in-law over Lucy's cradle, to whose loving care the dying Magdalen Filippini had recommended her child. Every time Canon Michael saw his little niece, he had a blessing and some small present for her. When taken to church on Sunday, she recognized him at the altar and listened quietly to his sermons. Lucy was hardly three years old when this other light was put out forever. Her saintly uncle Michael died, January 12, 1675, and was buried in the Cathedral church of Tarquinia. Four years later her own beloved father came to an untimely death. He died, having received all the Sacraments of the Church, on May 31, 1679, at the age of forty-eight, and was buried in the Church of St. Margaret in Tarquinia.

Seven years old and alone in the world! Lucy cried and prayed for her dear parents, feeling the great loss deeply but hardly realizing what it meant to be left without the love and affection, guidance and protection of father and mother so early in life. Being orphaned at such a tender age was regarded as a curse and a bad omen by pagan writers: "On whom parents have not smiled, him neither god has deemed worthy of his board nor goddess of her lodging."[5] But in Divine Revelation, a child of sorrow is a child of predilection. Sacred Scripture stresses God's gentle care of the fatherless. "Be merciful to the fatherless as a father."[6] "My father and my mother have left me, but the Lord hath taken me up."[7] Well could little Lucy, and her brother and her sister repeat those words of Scripture because the Lord did, from that moment, take paternal care of them all.

The Filippinis were well-to-do people. On their mother's

<hr>

[5] VIRGIL, 1. c., 62 f.
[6] Ecclus. 4:10.
[7] Ps. 26:10.

side, they were related to the first families of Tarquinia. The
father was not a native of Tarquinia. He had come with his
brother Michael from Vezzano Ligure in the old Republic of
Genoa. On the mother's side—the noble Picchi family—there
were four uncles and one aunt. One of the uncles, Anthony
Picchi, was married and had four young children, Anne, Mag-
dalene, Guido, and Catherine. Anne, the first of the children,
was born in 1672, the same year as her little cousin Lucy.

The three orphaned children could no longer remain in their
big paternal home. Their Uncle, Anthony Picchi, took them
into his home and cared for them so well that Lucy was often
regarded as a member of the Picchi family rather than of the
Filippinis, as it appears from some family documents of the
time.

A Christian home and the paternal hearth, the rallying place
of affections, are a paradise to a child and it is no small sacrifice to leave it at such a tender age. Home means heaven to an
innocent girl. It was here that little Lucy had learned to pray.
Here she had begun to honor God and our Blessed Lady, building little altars, bringing flowers and lighting candles to the
Infant Jesus and His Blessed Mother. It was here that she had
begun to examine her Angel-like conscience, asking forgiveness
for whatever little faults she thought she had committed. Going
down on her knees and joining her little hands she would say:
"Forgive me, please, for the love of God!" She would then go
to her room to kneel before her little altar and ask Jesus to pardon her. When the time for her first Sacramental Confession
had arrived, she spent hours preparing herself:

"What are you doing there?" asked Elizabeth, one day, seeing
her in that attitude.

"I am thinking of my sins."

"Sins!—What sins have you to need such a long examination?"

"Oh, you do not know how many faults we commit!"

This is the language of a tender and delicate conscience. Memories such as these were intimately connected with this home, with the rosy dreams of childhood days, and the dear ones who died there.

Little Lucy was now leaving this place with those memories in her soul.

The house in which she was born soon passed into other hands. In a generation or two the former owners—the Filippinis—were forgotten, so much so that the identity of that house remained a mystery until recently when it was finally identified by the coat of arms of that family. It is really the coat of arms of a Picchi, Lucy's mother, that appears painted in several places of the old palatial home.

The Religious Teachers Filippini—St. Lucy's spiritual daughters—have now acquired that building for their community. Thus, after nearly three hundred years, little Lucy has returned to her paternal home, the house where she loved to build little altars.

Her spiritual daughters have now built an altar in that house. On the altar they have placed the picture of a Saint, St. Lucy Filippini.

CHAPTER THREE

PUPIl AND TEACHER.

THE day arrived when the three orphaned children had to leave the house from which misfortune like a storm had swept their dearest ones away.

It has been said that souls once deeply wounded do not heal. The tender, sensitive soul of little Lucy had certainly been wounded in losing her father and leaving her home, but the Spirit of God had poured out a soothing balm on that secret wound, teaching her to turn misfortune into an occasion for virtue and for merit. Misfortune, according to St. Jerome, is never mournful to souls that accept it, for they always see that every cloud is an angel's face. Lucy accepted the great sacrifice and smiling through her tears left the big house with her brother and sister to go to uncle Anthony's home, her home for the next nine years.

Accepting cheerfully the new arrangement of Divine Providence, Lucy did everything in her power to show herself grateful to the relatives who had now become her foster parents. Obedient not only to every command given, she often anticipated the mere wishes of her relatives, performing spontaneously many menial duties that were both above her age and below her social station.

19

There was something in Lucy's natural temperament that inclined her to serve others. This natural instinct, ennobled by grace and guided by faith, later became the dynamic force of her apostolate, the characteristic and distinctive quality of her sanctity.

Lucy's Godward trend soon became manifest by her aversion to the little vanities and frivolities that mean much to an ordinary girl. She avoided the company of those whose words and actions were a scandal to others. Whenever she could warn the offending girl of the harm done to herself and to others by her conduct, she did so in all charity and humility.

Her sister Elizabeth was of a different temperament; she loved style and fashion with all their worldly vanities. She wore pretty dresses and fineries, and because of her social rank felt it was a duty to wear them.

Lucy looked at her older sister with a smile when she saw her decked out with ornaments. At the opportune moment she talked to her with much conviction and candor about the vanities of the world, the happiness that is found in serving God with a pure conscience, and the dangers that immodest dressing causes for a girl's virtue. Elizabeth took the lesson docilely and changed to more modest apparel. This crusade against immodest styles, started so early in life, was carried out with great success later in the numerous towns by her zeal and activity as teacher and missionary.

Lest one may think that the role of family censor assumed by young Lucy made her an unwelcome guest and companion, we quote from her earliest biographer: "She, Lucy, made her corrections with such sweetness and meekness as to cause her

"Forgive me, please, for the love of God!"

21

own sister to give up her vanities without any feeling of resentment in her heart."[1]

It takes so little for a child to be made happy: a flower, a toy, a sweet, a smile and all the tears are dried, all the worries forgotten. Lucy was still a child when she entered the new home where the tender care and the company of so many dear persons made her feel at ease again. Here she found a number of first cousins, all small, whose names we have already mentioned. Anne, the oldest of her cousins, was of her own age. They had been great friends before, now they looked at each other as real sisters. The two girls had the same ideals and pursued a common course in realizing them; detachment from worldly vanities and distractions, love of prayer, frequent and long visits to the churches of Tarquinia.

There was a very ancient Convent of Benedictine Nuns in the town, called the Convent of St. Lucy, attached to the church of the same name. The two girls, Lucy and Anne, paid frequent visits to this Convent which had a mysterious charm and attraction for their innocent souls. Lucy came here to pray to her heavenly Patron Saint, St. Lucy, Virgin and Martyr, and to talk with the good Nuns and be instructed by them. This was her first school. Among the Nuns were a few related to her on her mother's side; the noble ladies Donna Maria Magdalena Falzacappa, Donna Euphrasia Margarita Lucidi, and Costanza Maria Lucidi. All the Nuns had a tender love for the two pious girls, especially for the little orphan Lucy.

A boarding school was connected with the Convent, where the daughters of the better families of Tarquinia received a secular and religious education. As soon as Anne Picchi was old

---

[1] F. DI SIMONE. *Lucia Filippini.* Pag. 8.

enough, her father placed her in the school, so Lucy's visits to the Convent, became more frequent and more prolonged. The good spirit of her cousin Anne became manifest when from the boarding school she entered the Novitiate of the Benedictine Nuns. She made her Solemn Religious Profession there on February 25, 1690.

Breathing almost daily the religious atmosphere of the Convent, inspired by the example of virtue of so many saintly Nuns, young Lucy began to feel the mystical effects of the Beatitude that consists in hunger and thirst after justice and holiness. The time for her first Holy Communion came and she disposed herself for her first meeting with Jesus by a long and careful preparation. As a matter of fact her life so far had been such a preparation.

It was customary then as it is today in the city of Tarquinia to gather all the young girls, preparing for Holy Communion, in a Sisters' Convent for a retreat of a few days before the great event. Lucy and her cousin Anne, being of the same age, probably made their First Communion together under the direction of the Benedictine Nuns in the Church of St. Lucy.

The First Communion of a future Saint is a mystery that no human language can adequately explain. Baptism, Confirmation, Communion, these are the Sacraments that complete the mystical initiation, by effecting, in a sacramental way, spiritual purgation from sin, illumination of grace, perfect and real union with Christ, Our God and Savior. Holy Communion is the third and final step in Christian initiation; in it we receive the best that Faith can give in this life to man. Future life will reveal that He, whom we receive in Holy Communion is the same Lord who constitutes the eternal and all-transcending bliss of the Saints in Heaven. The bread of heaven is tasted both by Angels and men. Men taste it under the material species of bread and wine in the cloud of faith, the Angels in the light of glory in a face-to-face vision. To both men and Angels it is the bread of life, whose source is Jesus Himself, the Way, the Truth, and the Life.

Strengthened by this heavenly food, Lucy faced with more confidence the problems of life, especially now in the impressionable years of the approaching adolescence.

To a God-loving soul such problems cause no confusion or perplexity. The closer a Christian approaches God by love the simpler grows the gaze of the intelligence, the keener and clearer the vision. Lucy began to experience this soon after her first Communion.

She had always listened with rapt attention to the explanation of Christian doctrine given by her Pastor, every Sunday, in the school of Catechism. Her intelligence which was above average was greatly increased by her love of God, which alone in matters of Faith acts like a supernatural light. She often came out of school with a radiant expression of joy, showing the great satisfaction and contentment she experienced in listening to the explanation of the truths of Faith. She not only memorized her lessons but was always ready to explain them with a clarity and exactness that surprised not only her fellow pupils but the teacher himself. It was obvious that Lucy had been meditating on those eternal truths all during the week, carrying them in her mind and in her heart.

Her skill in Catechism was such that the Pastor finally gave her the honor of instructing younger girls in Christian Doctrine. This marked the beginning of her teaching career and her apostolate, and her aptitudes and inclinations became so manifest that her future vocation was unmistakable.

Young Lucy Explaining the Catechism

Lucy had listened always with great interest and with love to the lessons of Catechism. She began now to make those same lessons very interesting and attractive to her pupils. She had a special devotion to the sacred Passion of Christ whose mysteries she often explained to her class. She did this in so touching and convincing manner that tears came to the eyes of the young girls, as reported by Di Simone, who wrote that "more abundant were the tears that fell from the eyes of the pupils than the words that came from the mouth of their teacher."[2] Tears shed for such noble reasons humanize and purify the soul of young or old. Lucy had the special gift of touching the heart of her listeners. The marked success she attained in her school of Religion was proof enough of her mastery of the subject and of her teaching abilities. The power of teaching is, according to Aristotle, the one exclusive sign of a thorough knowledge. It is true that not every good student makes a good teacher, but it is equally true that there never was a good teacher who had not been a good student. Lucy Filippini had proved to be a proficient student; now she turned out to be an efficient teacher. One could detect even then another important quality in this young teacher of Religion in her early teens, her saintliness. People could have called her even then what the world called her in later years: *La Maestra Santa*—the saintly teacher.

Lucy's sixteenth birthday was not far off. Her cousin Anne had by this time expressed her desire to join the Benedictine Community after her graduation. Lucy wished nothing better than to follow the example of her cousin and of her maternal aunts, and spend the rest of her life as a Benedictine Nun in the Convent of St. Lucy. There were no financial difficulties to

[2] Op. cit., page 10.

prevent carrying out this desire. The required dowry had been assigned to her at the death of her parents, to be used either for her marriage or for her religious profession, as she chose.

The fact that such dowry existed can be gathered from an official document written much later in life—at the age of forty-six—by St. Lucy herself. This important document, which is found in her Process of Beatification, contains precious informations and reveals the great charity of Lucy Filippini. The document in full is translated here from the original Italian.

Montefiascone, November 14, 1718

I, the undersigned, being well advanced in years, and firmly resolved neither to become a nun nor to marry but to live in my present state as a Teacher until death, by the grace of God and in virtue of this my holograph, on the exclusive title of charity, do hereby renounce the whole amount of the Dowry which years ago was allocated to my person, and I do assign the same to one honest girl named Catherine Valentini, a poor orphan brought up in our schools by our Teachers, in order that said amount of money may not remain idle in the *S. Monte di Pietà* of the City of Corneto but serve as dowry to the said girl of Corneto, and this should serve as a title thereof.

In faith, etc.

I Lucia Filippini M.a pp.a

This beautiful document made in favor of a poor orphan girl from Corneto Tarquinia by one who herself had been left orphan of both parents so early in life speaks for itself. The words "firmly resolved neither to become a nun nor to marry" *—Con ferma risoluzione di non monacarmi, nè maritarmi—*

should not be understood as implying an aversion or dislike for the cloister. A dowry was needed for two specific purposes: marriage or religious profession. As long as Lucy had chosen neither of these states in life, the dowry could not be touched. Now that she was advanced in years and Divine Providence had opened a new field of activity and a new state in life, that of a Religious Teacher, she could legally dispose of her dowry in favor of a poor girl.

At the age of sixteen Lucy did not intend to spend her life as a teacher. Her heart longed for the peace and silence of the cloister, for the joy of contemplation in the House of God. As a matter of fact, when her true vocation—that of a Religious Teacher—was made manifest to her later, she became dangerously sick, yet, always obedient to the will of God, she joyfully embraced the cross and entered the way which the Lord had prepared for her. This had been always her real vocation in which she was to attain great sanctity and eternal glory. No doubt, her pious desire for a cloistered life was from God, but it was not to be regarded as a sign of her vocation; it was rather a preparation for it.

There are cases of conditional or temporary vocations. These are calls to a state which serves as a school and a preparation for another. The vocation of a teacher implies many distracting duties and situations. In order not to be carried away by such distractions and trials the soul must be well established in God. Love of solitude, of silence, of contemplation in a teacher should be regarded as a special grace given by God to recall her soul to Himself, in order to give her peace and rest and courage in the midst of her distractions, rather than a call to a cloistered life.

Knowing the further developments in Lucy's life, it may be

that such was the nature of her call to a sheltered and contemplative life.

As she approached her sixteenth birthday, rumors of the wonderful deeds performed by the new Bishop of Montefiascone and Corneto Tarquinia began to circulate in her home town. People spoke of his sanctity, his zeal, his charity, of the missions given in the town of Montefiascone and of similar ones to be started in Tarquinia before the arrival of the new Bishop, Cardinal Marcantonio Barbarigo, on January 25, 1688.

Lucy awaited the arrival of Cardinal Barbarigo, feeling in her heart that in this saintly Prelate she would meet a man of Divine Providence.

CHAPTER FOUR

SPIRITUAL FATHER AND GUIDE.

Aʙᴏᴜᴛ a year before Lucy's father died, Pope Innocent XI nominated the saintly Venetian Canon, Marcantonio Barbarigo, to the Archiepiscopal See of the island of Corfù in the Ionian Sea.

While preparing himself by a spiritual retreat for the episcopal consecration, Canon Barbarigo wrote a long list of resolutions and norms that were to guide his conduct as Bishop.

"Having been called by Divine Providence to be a Bishop—as my spiritual director assures me—I know that it will please that same Providence if I attend with all my heart to my own spiritual perfection, to the perfection of my Clergy, and to the salvation of the people committed to my care."

Of special interest for our story are his resolutions concerning the teaching of Christian Doctrine.

"First of all, I shall try to convince with sermons and pastoral letters all the fathers of families, tutors, administrators, and other superiors of the duty they have to learn and to teach Christian Doctrine, or to have others teach it in their name, both to their children and to their subjects. To this effect I shall give them the necessary books on Christian Doctrine and see to it that they teach it in all the churches and all the homes.

Cardinal Marcantonio Barbarigo

"I shall do everything in my power in order to oblige all schoolteachers to explain Christian Doctrine, beginning always with this sacred work before starting any other subject, such as reading, writing, grammar, etc."

"The Confessors, on finding culpable ignorance in this regard, shall impose as salutary penance the attending of classes of Catechism, both learning it and teaching it to others. If this penance has not been carried out for a considerable time, the Confessors according to their prudence shall defer the absolution."[1]

This extraordinary interest in the teaching of Christian Doctrine was not new in the life of Canon Barbarigo. Ever since his ordination to the priesthood, the teaching of Catechism to young and old had been his mission, the main work of his apostolate, first in the city of Venice, his birthplace, then in Padua, and now in Rome itself.

Born of a noble family in Venice on March 6, 1640, he gave early in life evident signs of piety and purity of conscience. He always practiced Christian mortification, learning to live on one simple meal a day and drinking only water, giving to the poor whatever he denied to his own needs and comforts. At twenty-five he became a member of the Grand Council of the Venetian Republic, but five years later he parted with the toga of his office to don the Ecclesiastical garment of a cleric in order to prepare for the priesthood. An exemplary priest from the day of his ordination, he worked unceasingly and unsparingly for the glory of God and His Church and the salvation of souls. He was one of the great moral figures of his century, both a great

---

[1] G. MARANGONI. *Card. Marcantonio Barbarigo.* Pag. 41 ff.

admirer and faithful imitator of St. Charles Borromeo and St. Francis de Sales.

This man Divine Providence had destined to be Lucy Filippini's spiritual father and guide, to interest her in what had always been his own mission, the teaching of Christian Doctrine to young and old, and to give her practical rules for a community of teachers, supporting her materially and morally all his life.

Yet, this man was now to be consecrated bishop of the vacant Archiepiscopal see of Corfù, in those days a possession of the Republic of Venice. Had one known God's plans regarding Lucy's future he might have wondered at such a turn as this, thinking perhaps that those plans had been changed. Nothing is more mysterious in this world than the ways of Divine Providence: "The heart of man disposeth his way, but the Lord must direct his steps."[2]

Marcantonio Barbarigo was consecrated Bishop in the Church of Santa Maria in Vallicella in Rome by another Barbarigo, the Blessed Cardinal Gregory Barbarigo, and soon after his consecration left Italy and reached Corfù on September 24, 1678, where he took possession of his Archdiocese.

His ardent zeal found a vast field of action for those apostolic works he had resolved on in the prayerful days of his retreat in Rome. There was no seminary on the island of Corfù when he arrived there. At his own expenses he built one and staffed it with competent teachers. His well-known program for the teaching of Christian Doctrine was carried out to the letter all over the island, and even aboard the Venetian fleet which often spent the winter months in the ports of Corfù. A fearful plague

[2] Prov. 16:9.

that broke out among the Venetian soldiers returning from their victorious campaign of Saint Maura gave Archbishop Barbarigo a new opportunity to display his heroic charity in the service of the sick and the dying, imitating in this the example of St. Charles Borromeo during the plague of Milan. This happened during the year 1684. Less than one year later he was called upon to prove to the world another of his virtues and another aspect of his noble character, the virtue of fortitude in defending the honor and the authority of the Church against the proud interference of lay usurpation.

The Venetian fleet was anchored in the ports of Corfù during the winter months of 1685. On the first Sunday in Lent that year the supreme Commander of that fleet, General Francesco Morosini, had the audacity of ordering his soldiers to remove the Archiepiscopal throne and carpet from the sanctuary of the Cathedral in order to place there his own chair and prie-dieu. His intention was to show all that he, Morosini, took precedence over the Archbishop, even in his own Cathedral, in the very sanctuary, in front of the altar. As this was being done in spite of remonstrations, Archbishop Barbarigo gave orders to have the announced exposition of the Blessed Sacrament that afternoon cancelled, to put out the candles, and for the Clergy to leave the church and not to be available for any function.

General Morosini arrived in full regalia with a retinue of officers and friends. He found the Cathedral empty and the lights out. Entering the sanctuary, he sat down in his chair, gave orders to have the candles lighted and the function started. Soon, however, he realized that no priests, not even the sexton, were to be found.

Morosini understood and, rising from his chair, threatened to hang the sexton and every Canon of the Cathedral. As for the Archbishop, that same evening, he received a letter which begins with these words:

"Extremely scandalous and insolent was your action, Most Reverend Barbarigo, in this Cathedral church, a few moments ago. . . ."

The letter concludes with a command for the Archbishop to leave the island of Corfù with the first available boat and return to the Dominante—Venice—there to present himself to the Grand Council in order to receive the punishment he deserved.[3]

Barbarigo remained a few months in Corfù and in the meantime he informed the Holy See of the unhappy incident with Morosini. He finally went to Venice but only for a very short time and without presenting himself to the Grand Council. From there he went to Rome.

The Venetian Senate, which regarded Morosini as the heroic conqueror of Peloponnesus, began a merciless prosecution of Marcantonio Barbarigo trying him *"in absentia"* and depriving him of all the revenues of the Archiepiscopal office and all the fruits of his personal patrimony. Barbarigo was thus reduced to real poverty. The Holy Father gave him an apartment in the palace of the Cancelleria in Rome with a small pension for his support.

[3] G. MARANGONI, op. cit., page 104, f. From a letter written to the Doge by Arch. Barbarigo, during the following month of March, with the purpose of explaining the incident with Morosini, it appears that Morosini had always treated Barbarigo with scorn. He had insisted that the Archbishop walk always on Morosini's left and always give him the place of honor, and to meet him at the church door whenever he went to Mass. Another proud Venetian, Girolamo Cornaro, was Governor of Cortù at this time. He, too, interfered so much with Barbarigo that the latter was forced to absent himself from the island for nearly two years. It was time, therefore, to give a lesson to such people and defend the honor and the authority of the Church.

On the morning of September 2, 1686, Archbishop Barbarigo was praying in the Church of San Lorenzo in Damaso annexed to the Cancelleria, assisting at several Masses and asking our Lord to come to his assistance amidst his trials and afflictions. That very morning his prayers were heard. He was still kneeling in the church when he was notified that the Pope had created him Cardinal in the consistory held that morning. This great honor came as a complete surprise to him who had never sought any honor or dignity except that of serving God. Seeing in this act of the Holy Father a solemn justification of his conduct in the past painful incidents of Corfù, he wept before God and once more dedicated his life to the service and glory of God and His Church.

Barbarigo was given the Cardinal title to the Church of St. Susanna in Rome. Eleven years later, his differences with the Venetian Republic having been settled, his title was changed to that of St. Marc, which was ordinarily the title reserved for a Venetian Cardinal.

About one year after his elevation to the Cardinalate he was made Ordinary of the united dioceses of Montefiascone and Corneto Tarquinia; (today Tarquinia is united to Civitavecchia, Montefiascone to Acquapendente). Towards the end of October of 1687 he entered Montefiascone where he was received as an Angel from heaven. His coming marks the beginning of a new era for that diocese, an era of spiritual revival, moral and social restoration, whose lasting effects are noticeable even today.

The social, religious, and moral conditions were extremely sad throughout the whole diocese at this time. These conditions were the result of several causes, chief among them being the paganizing influence of the Italian Renaissance; the disregard of the law of residence on the part of bishops; the lack of neces-

Lucy's First Meeting with Cardinal Barbarigo

sary formation for the clergy; the scandalous conduct of prince-
ly families ruling over those towns; the ignorance and worldliness of priests and religious; unrestrained licentiousness in
men and women. This period was also one of cultural decadence, in which flourished such false and exaggerated doctrines
and practices as Jansenism and Quietism.

This is the century in which Lucy grew up and became a
Saint. The man whom the Pope had sent to rule the Church of
Corfù was brought back by Divine Providence at an opportune
time, in order to head a diocese in dire need of reform and to
become the spiritual guide of a future Saint. Lucy was now
sixteen years old, an age in need of direction and guidance
especially for one bereaved of her parents.

Towards the end of January of 1688, Cardinal Barbarigo
made his first pastoral visit to Tarquinia. His coming was no
mere formality. It was to be the beginning of a visible change
in the religious and moral life of the people of that town. Before his coming, a mission had been preached in Tarquinia lasting nearly five weeks. Lucy made this mission with customary
diligence and with extraordinary spiritual profit. She succeeded
in bringing her sister Elizabeth to make the mission with the
proper spirit, not as an occasion for displaying her new dresses
but to adorn her soul with virtue and grace.

The Cardinal arrived just at the time to reap the fruits of
that long mission. He personally distributed more than two
thousand Holy Communions in a town of some 2300 inhabitants. In the afternoon he himself carried the Blessed Sacrament in solemn procession throughout Tarquinia, followed by
a large and devout crowd of faithful.

Cardinal Barbarigo took notice not only of the general needs
of the parishes in that town but also of particular families and

persons. He listened patiently to each of his spiritual children; the poorest and most neglected were singled out for his special care and attention; he established a school of Catechism in every Parish church of Tarquinia.

In connection with the special work of his pastoral care—the teaching of Catechism—the name of a young lady, Lucy Filippini, must have been brought up by the curate of the church in which Lucy had been teaching Christian Doctrine for the last few years. The Cardinal expressed the desire to meet this young teacher whose virtue and zeal were praised by all in Tarquinia.

The same Divine Spirit that had made of Barbarigo an apostle of Christian Doctrine and of Lucy an efficient teacher of Catechism thus brought these two souls together. The plans of Divine Providence never fail, even when they seem to travel in a direction opposite to their real goal. Witness Barbarigo's first appointment to Corfù.

Lucy herself had greatly desired to talk to this man of God. When Saints meet there is hardly need of introduction. They seem to know and to understand each other very well from the first moment. Their souls are perfectly attuned to the same Divine Spirit. In the present meeting there was another common element: both were actively interested in Christian Doctrine. Common interests create mutual understanding.

Lucy's demeanor on this occasion, her piety and innocence, so manifest in the cloudless serenity of her youthful face and the clear light of her eyes, made a deep impression on the Cardinal.

"May I talk with your parents, young lady?" asked the Cardinal.

A cloud passed over her face; for a moment, the light in her eyes went out.

"My parents are with God, Your Eminence!" replied Lucy, bravely controlling her tears.

"My child, a Bishop must be a father to the orphan. I therefore will take care of your education and eventually place you in that state of life which you, with the grace of God, shall choose for yourself."

Lucy accepted the generous offer of the Cardinal with gratitude, but she realized at once that this meant her leaving Tarquinia, her own brother and sister, and her foster parents. She was ready for the sacrifice but the thought of her sister, left behind in the midst of dangers and temptations, made her hesitate a little.

The Cardinal understood.

"Your sister is an orphan like yourself, my child, and I must be a father to her as well," replied the Cardinal.

Lucy was now really happy, and she knelt to kiss the Cardinal's ring.

"God reward Your Eminence for so much charity and kindness!"—said Lucy after kissing the ring.

It was agreed, with the consent of Lucy's uncle Anthony Picchi, to send Elizabeth, now nineteen years old, to the boarding school of the Benedictine Sisters of Tarquinia to complete her education, and to place Lucy in the Convent school of St. Clare in Montefiascone. The Cardinal took personal care of the expenses, not touching a penny of the girls' dowry. Lucy's brother John Francis, who was now twenty-two years old, was taken care of by the estate left by his parents.

The pastoral visitation of Tarquinia took several days, after which the Cardinal visited one after another the other towns of his territory. During these several months Lucy prepared herself for a life away from home. When the time finally arrived she quietly left the house, and walked down the narrow streets towards the northern gate of the city, called Porta Firenze. Just outside this gate is a lovely valley called Valverde—Green Valley—sloping gently towards the seashore. In this valley is an ancient Shrine of the Blessed Virgin Mary, honored for centuries as the Madonna of Valverde.

Ever since her childhood Lucy had felt attracted to this church. It was here that she first understood that the Mother of Jesus was truly her own mother and felt an orphan no longer. She often came here with he rsister Elizabeth and her cousin Anne, but whenever her heart was heavy she came alone and spoke to the sweet Madonna and her Divine Infant as a child to her mother.

On this occasion her heart was heavy at the thought that this visit was her last. She wanted to say so many things but her heart would not let her. She wept silently out of love and gratitude at the feet of the Madonna. Again she dedicated herself to the service of Jesus and Mary and asked them for their blessing.

As Lucy looked up, the beautiful Madonna, in the attitude of inviting the Divine Infant to bless, seemed to come alive and to smile, and she knew that both little Jesus and His Mother had actually blessed her as she said: *"Nos cum Prole pia benedicat Virgo Maria!"*—She was now ready for the sacrifice of leaving all for the love of God.

The Filippini orphan children were finally separated from one another. For the first time in her life, Lucy left her home town. She did so without tears in her eyes but not without pain in her heart. Old wounds bled again as family ties were torn anew. She left behind the graves of father and mother and of the uncle priest who had baptized her. It seems strange that after so many years she would have felt their absence at this juncture so keenly. There were no parents there to bless her at this moment, but the whole town of Tarquinia blessed her name for the example of virtue she left there. One day they are to bless and acclaim her as the citizens of Bethulia acclaimed Judith: "Thou art the honor of our people! . . . The hand of the Lord hath strengthened thee, and therefore thou shalt be blessed forever!"[4]

Barbarigo's promise to take care of Elizabeth's future was carried out generously. Having completed her education at the Cardinal's expenses, she married a distinguished gentleman named Francesco Bonifazi, at whose death Elizabeth came in possession of a rich inheritance. She was thus in a position to assist her sister, when after the death of Cardinal Barbarigo Lucy ran into financial difficulties with her schools because of an unscrupulous administrator. Elizabeth was married a second time after the death of her first husband, this time to Ludovico Ciucci. She died on November 21, 1741, nine years after Lucy's death. She asked to be buried next to her in the Cathedral of Montefiascone.

[4] Judith, 15:10 f.

CHAPTER FIVE

FORMATION AND VOCATION.

LUCY waited until Cardinal Barbarigo had completed the
pastoral visitation of the entire diocese and reentered Montefiascone before leaving for St. Clare's Convent School.

Early one morning in the month of July of 1688, accompanied
by some relatives, she left Tarquinia by coach.

The winding road first reached the little town of Vetralla,
known as *Forum Cassii* by the Romans. Here it entered the old
Roman highway, the *Via Cassia*, where turning left, it ran north
towards Viterbo, the city of the Popes and St. Rose. Just before
reaching Viterbo, a short distance off the Cassian highway is the
celebrated Shrine of the Blessed Virgin Mary: *Santa Maria
della Quercia*, the goal of many of Lucy's devout pilgrimages
during her whole life. Time did not permit her to stop on this
occasion but her heart was at the feet of the dear Madonna all
the while. Our Lady of Valverde in Tarquinia must have assured her the day before, when she found the parting so hard:
Wherever you go, my child, your Mother goes with you!

The party probably stopped for awhile in Viterbo during the
hours of intense summer heat of the early afternoon. Soon after
resuming their journey northward, their road began to climb a
little. Far in the distance loomed a picture of grandeur and
beauty, the dome of the Cathedral of Montefiascone. The town

43

itself, built on an elevation of two thousand feet, southeast of
Lake Bolsena, offers a view that can hardly be matched for
vastness and beauty. Two of the most ancient roads cross on
top of the hill on which the town of Montefiascone is located.
At this crossing the old Etruscans are said to have erected the
temple of Voltumna, the federal center of Etruria. The first
settlement must have started around this ancient pagan shrine.
The present prosaic name of Montefiascone is probably a corruption of *Montisfalisci,* the Latin name of the place being *Falis-
codunum.*[1]

Lucy could hardly take her eyes from that inspiring vision,
the octagonal cupola of the Cathedral like a golden crown,
dominating the whole town and the countryside. Something
fascinated her in that vision. Had perhaps the indwelling Spirit
revealed something of her future?—This was the town where
most of her life on earth would be spent—here she would close
the course of her days—under that majestic cupola her mortal
remains would await the day of resurrection—that same town
and church would, one day—today—have a new Patron Saint:
St. Lucy Filippini! No, this glorious future, most probably, remained enshrouded in mystery for her, but that joyful feeling of
going home, which she experienced on entering Montefiascone,
told her that this was the place where God wanted her. She
thanked the Lord for calling her to such a picturesque town
whose sight eased the pain she felt on leaving lovely Tarquinia.

It is said that geographical location is responsible—to a great

[1] How from the word *Falisci* came *fiascone* (a large, pear-shaped wine
bottle) may be explained perhaps by the shape of the mountain on
which the town is built and from the excellent muscatel wine produced
there, a wine very popular in Rome under the name of: EST, EST, EST.

extent—for man's activity and behavior, on the purely natural plane. A beautiful and inspiring location cannot itself alone be the cause of good deeds nor prevent man from falling into grave sin. Neither the glory of Heaven nor the beauty and happiness of the Garden of Eden were a sufficient guaranty against sin and misery for either angel or man. Yet, the fact remains that, under the influence of grace, a beautiful and inspiring location can become an extrinsic factor in the performance of great and glorious deeds.

Late that July afternoon, Lucy reached Montefiascone and went straight to the Convent of St. Clare where Cardinal Barbarigo had made arrangements for her admission as a boarding pupil.

It was thus that Lucy was first introduced into a Franciscan atmosphere. The name itself of St. Clare—the little plant of St. Francis—must have evoked feelings of devotion and admiration in her soul.

Even though this Convent of St. Clare was by no means a cloistered community of nuns it was nevertheless a religious community dedicated to St. Clare of Assisi whose example of heroic virtue the Sisters strived to imitate.

This particular community had been started by a zealous Capuchin, named Father Modestus of Ruviano, following a mission he gave in Montefiascone in 1630. A number of young ladies fired by his word and anxious to do penance for their sins or to protect their virtue from the dangers of the world, begged the good Father to guide and direct them in a spiritual and virtuous life. A modest building was acquired near the church of St. Clare and there a sort of religious community was started under the official title of *The Purgatory of St. Clare*. The title well explains the purpose of the community, to do penance and to purge their souls from sin. They observed extreme poverty in all things and this in itself gave the Sisters a constant opportunity for mortification and penance. St. Clare must have loved this community which tried to imitate the example of evangelical poverty she had practiced at San Damiano in Assisi. In the year 1636, the Bishop of Montefiascone approved both the spirit and the form of this community, giving them special rules to follow and appointing one of them as their superior. He also changed the official title from *Purgatory* to *Conservatory of St. Clare.*

The saintly life of these first sisters did not fail to attract the attention of the leading families of the city who frequently visited the Convent with great spiritual profit. In the course of time they expressed the desire that the Sisters make it possible for young ladies of the city to go there for religious and secular education. Having first obtained the Bishop's permission, the Sisters opened a boarding school for young ladies of the better families of Montefiascone (the poor were given no opportunity for school education in those days) and neighboring towns. Some of these pupils joined the community later as Sisters.

The boarding school brought a sort of prosperity to the poor community which began slowly to raise its own standard of living. The Sisters changed their former penitential garb for a more comfortable dress; one after another the works of penance and the spiritual exercises of the community were eliminated till there was no community life left. This has been often the case with Religious Orders which changed to teaching entirely when their original purpose was different. It did not take long for the people of Montefiascone to notice the change. They were scandalized and with subtle irony nicknamed the Sisters: *Monachelle*—Little Nuns—a nickname which still remains regardless of many reforms that have taken place since that time. However, the relaxation from the former spirit did not affect all the members of the community. There still remained a number of Sisters who retained unchanged their former fervor and spirit. Some of these—very advanced in years—were still living when Lucy entered the Convent school.

The vicissitudes of the religious community were of little concern to Lucy who had come there with high ideals of perfection. To be out of the vanities and corruption of the world was paradise to her. The worldliness of some teachers did not affect her, for she looked always to those who lived close to God and gave edification by their virtuous life.

A little room—a convent cell—was assigned to her. It had a small window, a little desk, a narrow and hard bed, above which was a picture of St. Clare. Underneath the picture the following words were written:

"I, Clare, the servant of Jesus Christ, and the little plant of our Father Saint Francis, your sister and your mother, however unworthy, pray our Redeemer, that by the intercession of His Most Holy Mother, of Saint Michael the Archangel, of the Holy Angels, and all the Saints to give you and confirm you in this holy blessing in heaven and on earth: on earth by increasing in you His grace and strength, in heaven by raising you to be among His saints."

"While still living I give you my benediction, as far as I can, and beyond what I can. Amen."[2]

Among Lucy's books must have been the Life of St. Clare of Assisi, the Fioretti of St. Francis and other documents of the Franciscan spirit. It was during her years of formation in this

[2] NESTA DE ROBECK. *St. Clare of Assisi, The Benediction of St. Clare.* Pag. 178.

house that she acquired the truly Franciscan love for evangelical poverty, the cheerful spirit that made her sing in the midst of trials and afflictions, the selfless love for the little ones, the needy, the afflicted. She must have read many times that precious fragment of St. Francis' last letter to St. Clare:

"I Francis, the Little Brother, desire to follow the life and the poverty of our highest Lord Jesus Christ until the end. And I entreat you, my ladies, and counsel you to abide always by the most holy way of life and abide in poverty. And be most watchful that you never recede from it by the advice and counsel of others."[3]

Among the remaining devout members of that Religious community there was a certain Sr. Lucia Frangiotti who must have inspired our Lucy both by her words of wisdom and her luminous example.

Lucy's innocence and great purity of conscience soon became manifest to all. They regarded her as the angel of the Convent. Angelic were Lucy's words of comfort and encouragement, angelic her conduct with teachers and fellow students, angelic and seraphic her behavior in church. Her first biographer tells us that she tried always to comfort everyone who was troubled and afflicted and that the grace of God would always second her pious intentions so well that people found real relief and solace in her words.

True to her natural inclination to work and make herself useful at all times, she applied herself constantly to manual or mental work thus keeping her soul and her senses always engaged,

[3] OTTO KARRER, *St. Francis of Assisi,* The Writings of Brother Leo and His Companions, 105 (143).

shunning idleness of which Scripture says that "idleness has taught much evil."[4]

By working, watching, and praying she overcame the common temptations of those impressionable years, keeping her soul untarnished and pure. The example of her virtue and the charm of her manners did not remain hidden within the Convent walls and soon the noble ladies of the city asked the Sisters to allow them to meet young Lucy Filippini and talk to her. She consented graciously, seeing in this an opportunity for Catholic Action, thus beginning that mission for good which in one form or another was to continue for life. Her manners were edifying and charming but without affectation. They were a natural expression of her soul, of her fine character enhanced by the grace of God and the gifts of the Holy Spirit, for sanctity has a charm of its own.

None of her biographers tell us anything about her studies, either at the Convent School or previously in Tarquinia, so she must have received the ordinary school education prevalent in those days. The only allusion made to school matters at this point is that Lucy found some of the Sisters in St. Clare's Convent who were unable to read and write and that she in her charity took upon herself the task of teaching them.

Lucy had taken a trunk or two of clothes and fineries to the Convent school for her personal use, but she kept everything locked up in a chest being satisfied with a simple school uniform. Her delicate conscience even found ground for sorrow and shame for keeping those vanities in her room.

"To what purpose do you accuse yourself of vanity in confession," she would say, "when you keep vain ornaments in

[4] Ecclus. 33:29.

your cell? Get rid of them all! It is not easy to stay close to a fire and not be burned, nor is it difficult for you to keep these ornaments in your room and not to wear them sometimes. You accuse yourself of vanity, but your confession to be good must remove not only sin but also the occasion of sin."[5]

Cardinal Barbarigo frequently called at St. Clare's Convent and school where he watched with great interest Lucy's progress in virtue and studies. He called her affectionately "my daughter." Lucy in her turn venerated him as a saint and loved him as a father, depending entirely on his advice.

Nearly four years had passed since she had come to Montefiascone. Her education, according to the standards of the time, was more than complete. She was twenty years old and it was time to choose a vocation. The pious Cardinal left this important decision entirely to her choice. She prayed to the Holy Ghost, she asked her heavenly Mother for light and guidance in such an important matter. Her heart inclined to the solitude of the cloister and the peace of contemplation more than ever, yet she was prudent enough to understand that the inner inclination is not always a dependable sign of vocation. Her God-given aptitudes of mind and body, her temperament and character were made to serve, to work, and to lead an apostolic life of activity. These actually were the signs of her true vocation. She did not know what kind of service and what activity her gifts were meant for. There was some indecision and struggle in her mind before the voice of obedience told her formally what service, what duties would be hers for life. That voice actually revealed her vocation, the vocation of a religious teacher. This was the will of God in her regard. It took

[5] F. DI SIMONE, op. cit., page 14.

quite awhile for her to convince herself of it. She suffered because her vocation would necessarily bring her back into the world with its distractions. Her spiritual guide the pious Cardinal, enlightened her on this point: she would go into the world as an apostle, to save it for Christ.

CHAPTER SIX

TWO TEACHERS—TWO SYSTEMS.

No lasting moral reform of society has ever been possible without systematic instrucion, without a school. Cardinal Barbarigo was fully aware of this when he started the reform of his diocese by opening of a new Seminary for Clerics, with additional facilities for the Christian education of other young men of his diocese, who did not intend to enter the priesthood. Having happily carried out this part of his program, in the year 1690, he turned his mind to opening free schools for girls in every town of his diocese.

The school system then differed widely from what was introduced in almost every nation of Europe during the nineteenth century at a time when education became secularized and a subsidy of the State. There was undoubtedly an invasion of family rights, for the education of children is indeed a public interest but not necessarily a public utility such as level of gas, light, and transportation. It is true that without the compulsory measures adopted by civil authority in making school attendance obligatory for all, many among the poorer classes stayed away from school and grew up without any school education. The remedy of secularized schools, offered by the State, did not make things better for society. Humanity may have become more educated in the last century but not better. A century ago, the great Italian writer Tommaseo, who witnessed the suppression of many private schools, said: "When a school ceases to be a temple, it becomes a den." Time has proved how right he was.

The school of the seventeenth century was almost universally a school for the upper class, and education was regarded as a privilege of the nobility and the well-to-do. The poor people —always in the majority—could not afford the price of even elementary education.

Cardinal Barbarigo realized that the sad moral conditions prevailing in his diocese were, to a great extent, the result of ignorance. "Considering how much a good education of women and especially of young girls would contribute to the general welfare of the entire diocese and to the sound Christian living of the whole family, he thought of opening schools for them, first in Montefiascone and then in every town of his diocese."[1]

He needed a goodly number of teachers for these schools but he had none. His plan was to use the first school to be opened in Montefiascone as a sort of preparatory school and novitiate for teachers, where, in addition to the elementary training, such girls with the proper inclination and ability could be given special training to prepare them for their mission.

The Cardinal studied his plan for a long time, asking advice from persons experienced in this matter. He hired teachers from various places, some even from Rome, but these did not prove equal to the task and the undertaking failed.

While in this dilemma it happened one day, in 1692, that two Jesuit Fathers called on him while on their way through Montefiascone. The Cardinal received them graciously, and in

[1] G. MARANGONI. *Card. Marcantonio Barbarigo.* Pag. 163.

the course of their conversation, the subject of popular schools came up. He told them of his plan and the failure to find competent teachers. The two visitors told him the success Cardinal Facchinetti of Viterbo had had in this regard with the help of an able young teacher, Rose Venerini. This young person had been inspired and guided in her work first by her spiritual director, Father Martinelli, S.J., and later by another Jesuit, Father Moirani.

The Cardinal saw the hand of Divine Providence in this unexpected visit of the two Jesuits; it was an answer to his prayers. He sat down at his desk and wrote two letters, one to Father Moirani, S.J., asking him to have Miss Venerini come to Montefiascone and help him with his schools; another letter addressed to Rose Venerini herself, presented his problem to her, begging her to come to help him.

The Cardinal did not ask Rose Venerini to establish schools of her own diocese but to help him start his own diocesan schools with a complete program he had prepared. With the consent of her director, Rose Venerini accepted Cardinal Barbarigo's call, stating that she was lending her service to the Cardinal for a time, not indefinitely. She would return to her own schools of Viterbo as soon as a few teachers had been trained well enough. The Cardinal with Lucy Filippini in mind to take charge of his schools, as soon as she could be available, was not in the least disappointed by the condition Miss Venerini had attached. The Cardinal at once had Rose and one of her assistants brought to Montefiascone to choose a convenient house for the school. While the building was being adapted for use of the first teachers, Rose Venerini and her companion stayed at the Convent School of St. Clare.

It was here that the future St. Lucy Filippini and Blessed

Rose Venerini first met. Lucy was only twenty and an accomplished student, Rose was thirty-six and with some years of experience as a teacher. Miss Venerini was deeply impressed by the qualities of mind and heart of young Lucy so, when some time later she returned to Viterbo, she knew of no better person to recommend to the Cardinal to take the direction of his schools than Lucy Filippini.

The building was soon made ready and the first school opened in Montefiascone that same year 1692, only two years after the opening of the new Seminary. Only forty girls were admitted at first; more wished to come but Rose Venerini thought it better to limit this number in order to give these first comers the best possible training. A great change in the lives of these girls became evident after the first few weeks at school; there was more modesty, better knowledge of Christian doctrine, a more frequent and more devout reception of the Sacraments. The saintly Cardinal, real promoter of this work, was very happy at hearing of this initial success of his plan. He never tired of exhorting young women and housewives to come to this school where classes of Christian Doctrine were open to young and old.

Soon after Rose Venerini arrived in Montefiascone the Cardinal asked to be shown her program and her method. He approved part of it but made a number of changes which he wanted for his school. Rose did not like any changes in her own method and program; she complied at Montefiascone but never introduced the changes of the Cardinal into her own schools.

The Cardinal was extremely interested in seeing this school firmly established in order that graduates could serve as future teachers, to continue the work and extend it to other places.

Knowing that Rose Venerini would not remain for long he tried to induce Lucy, on whom he had his eye, as the real head of his future Institute, to come to a final decision on her vocation. Rose, no longer at St. Clare's Convent, paid frequent visits to Lucy to instruct her about her method and the subjects taught at the school, trying at the same time to win her for school work. At first, Lucy seemed inclined to accept Rose's suggestion, but her love of solitude and contemplation was still very strong in her soul. She was afraid of the constant and unavoidable distractions of a school, of the withering effect such a work can have on the spirit over a long period, and her soul seemed to retreat to the peaceful quiet of the cloister again. She begged Rose not to present her name to the Cardinal as a teacher. Rose, always determined and unchanging in her ways, paid no attention to Lucy's pleading, and convinced of her ability and excellent character, told the Cardinal that "in the whole city of Montefiascone Lucy was the only one who could be employed as teacher with profit of souls."[2]

The Cardinal himself must have pleaded with Lucy for quite some time before she made up her mind. The Cardinal's biographer G. Marangoni tells us that Barbarigo succeeded "not without much labor, charity, and patience in convincing Lucy, whose spirit was unwilling to live in the same school house with the teachers and to wear their uniform."[3]

Lucy finally consented, more out of deference to the Cardinal than from an inner conviction. She obeyed in the darkness of faith, sacrificing her strongest inclinations to the will of God. So she entered the career of a Religious Teacher, the road marked for her by Divine Providence, her true vocation. She

[2] F. DI SIMONE. *Lucia Filippini.* Pag. 20.
[3] G. MARANGONI, op. cit., page 168.

left the little cell where she had spent four peaceful years and where she had learned so much about the Little Poor Man of Assisi and his "little plant" St. Clare. These were practically the last peaceful years of her life, the years of her hidden life, her Nazareth.

The special dress worn by the teachers at the time was not the religious habit designed later by the Cardinal himself for his Religious Teachers, when they were organized into a community with proper rules, a community governed by Lucy Filippini.

Marangoni reports that as soon as sufficient teachers had been trained in the school at Montefiascone, the Cardinal sent Rose Venerini to open other schools in the larger towns of the diocese, the first being Tarquinia. According to Di Simone, however, and to local tradition, it was Lucy Filippini who actually opened all the other schools in the diocese for Cardinal Barbarigo. The two accounts may well agree if we acknowledge that the two saintly teachers went together to this first opening. This must be true about the school of Tarquinia, for although Lucy's name is not given by Andreucci, Rose Venerini's biographer, it is well understood from the context.[4]

Rose's return to Viterbo became urgent when disagreements and resentments developed among her teachers. All had left the schools except one. Rose humbly requested Cardinal Barbarigo to interpose with the major superiors of the Jesuits to obtain Father Martinelli's return to Viterbo as the only person who could cope with the critical situation of her schools. Barbarigo was only too happy to comply with her request and he actually succeeded in obtaining Father Martinelli's return.

Lucy now became the head of the teachers and all the schools

[4] A. G. ANDREUCCI. *Rosa Venerini.* Pag. 28.

of the Cardinal's diocese, living and teaching in the school of Montefiascone near the Cathedral church.

At this time, all the material elements of a teaching institute, later known as the Institute of the *Maestre Pie,* were present. The institute took its name from the spontaneous offer of young ladies to spend their life teaching Christian Doctrine and the rudiments of learning to young girls, with no other desire than the glory of God and the salvation of souls.

Because of Rose Venerini's assistance to Cardinal Barbarigo's school program, one writer has tried to defend the thesis that Rose Venerini was the real foundress of the *Maestre Pie*.[5] The constant tradition and official Papal documents are opposed to the opinion defended in such a thesis. A few of these documents are reported here.

There is first of all the *Apostolic Letter of Pope Clement XIII,* dated September 8, 1760, beginning with the words *Experientia rerum,* explaining the nature of the Institute and giving the name of Cardinal Barbarigo as the real founder.

"Experience—a teacher in all things—has given sufficient proof of how useful to the education of young girls has been the community of some Virgins called *Maestre Pie* whom Bishops have permitted to live together, under their jurisdiction, even though not bound by laws of enclosure nor by religious profession, to dedicate themselves exclusively to God and to

---

[5] This was done especially by Father Celi, S.J. in a series of articles entitled *Le Origini delle Maestre Pie,* published in the CIVILTA CATTOLICA from January, 1925, to February, 1926. A good answer to Celi's arguments was given by Dr. P. Bergamaschi in his book *Le Origini delle Maestre Pie,* Rome, 1926, and by Card. Carlo Salotti, in his biography *La Santa Lucia Filippini, Fondatrice e Superiora delle Maestre Pie,* Rome, 1930—the whole chapter VIII of this book should be read.

teach with diligence the principles of sincere piety and as well as handicraft to young girls, especially those of the poorer class, who either board with them or frequent their schools. . . ."

"This Pious Society (*Maestre Pie*) as we have been informed, was first founded by Cardinal Marco Barbarigo, our fellow citizen of happy memory, when he was Bishop of Montefiascone. . . ."

Another important document is the *Apostolic Letter of Pope Leo XII,* dated October, 1828, beginning with the words: *Praeter puerorum institutionem,* mentioned in the first chapter of this book. In this document the Pope commanded that the various families or branches of Maestre Pie existing at the time under the name of *Maestre Pie Filippini, Maestre Pie Venerini, Maestre Operaie,* and others, should be joined to form one Institute, governed by the same rules, but divided in two distinct families, one—The Maestre Pie Filippini—to be under the jurisdiction of the Pope's Almoner, the other—The Maestre Pie Venerini—under the jurisdiction of the Apostolic Datary.

The Holy See, in virtue of these documents, acknowledged Barbarigo as the common remote founder of the Institute of the *Maestre Pie;* the immediate foundress of the one family as St. Lucy Filippini, of the other, Blessed Rose Venerini.

Cardinal Bonaventura Garola, in a letter written August 8, 1821, to Cardinal Severoli, Bishop of Viterbo, called Cardinal Barbarigo "the first and most saintly Founder and Institutor of these *Maestre Pie Falische e Cornetane*—Religious Teachers of Montefiascone and Corneto Tarquinia." In another letter by the same Cardinal to the Superior of the Religious Teachers, dated September 24, 1829, he insisted, concerning their religious habit, they should keep the one given them by "Lucy Filippini, of happy memory, foundress of the *Scuole Pie*—Religious

Schools—with full approval of His Eminence Card. Barbarigo, our predecessor of happy and dear memory."[6]

During the process of Beatification of Lucy Filippini, an objection was raised against her title of *Foundress of the Maestre Pie*, because her first biographer, who wrote her life in 1732, the year she died, never gave her the title of Foundress. The objection was rejected as baseless, because during the past two centuries the Servant of God had been regarded as true Foundress so that her spiritual daughters, taking their name from her own family name, called themselves *Maestre Pie Filippini*.[7]

In the allocution given by Pope Pius XI, on March 21, 1926, mentioned in our Introduction, Lucy was called Foundress more than once: "Lucy Filippini, the Saintly Teacher, model and molder (*formatrice*) of saintly teachers. . . . And now after a long lapse of time she still remains the Saintly Teacher, the foundress (*fondatrice*) of saintly teachers. . . ."[8]

Differences of method and system did certainly exist but such differences were always consistent with charity, respect, and confidence in each other. As a matter of fact when Lucy thought of resigning as Superioress because of differences of view between herself and Cardinal Barbarigo about the new arrangement at St. Clare's Convent, to be seen later, she thought of joining the schools of Rose Venerini in Viterbo.[9] This certainly proves that between the two teachers there was unity of heart and soul regardless of differences of system and method. Some

[6] E. CHIERICHETTI, footnotes to Marangoni's Card. M. Barbarigo, page 326.
[7] Summarium. *Responsio ad Animadversiones R. P. D. Promotoris Fidei,* 47.
[8] C. SALOTTI, op. cit., page 341.
[9] Ibid. 125.

biographers have stressed these differences to make the two women appear antagonistic, and some of the expressions used by Rose Venerini might lend themselves to such interpretation. Each saint has a marked personality, each tending to the same goal but hardly ever by the same way and the same method.

Life in the school of Montefiascone was very much like that of a religious community. The future teachers lived together in a separate section of the school building under the direction and guidance of Lucy Filippini. She observed and studied each one closely, noticing their application to study and their moral conduct. They were taught the so-called three R's, as well as domestic sciences, Christian Doctrine, and the basic norms of sound Christian living so that they could efficiently teach others when the time came. Both teachers and pupils were under the spiritual direction of their Confessor whose assistance was limited to the confessional in the church. They ate at the same table, the teachers taking turns at reading during part of their meals. There was abstinence from meat on Wednesdays, as well as fasting on Fridays and Saturdays of each week. Not even a drink of water was allowed between meals without the Superior's permission. They wore a simple and modest black dress and low shoes.

The Cardinal provided for the expenses of the schools of the diocese, and for all the teachers. He exhorted his priests to urge the parents in their parishes to send their daughters to these schools. He also requested every Pastor to give him a list of all the girls of school age living in his parish, which he gave to the Principal of the respective school. They in turn were to get in touch with the family, requesting in the name of the Cardinal that the girls be sent to school. In order to encourage attendance at school among the girls of poor families, the Cardinal bought great quantities of material for spinning, such as flax, hemp, wool, allowing each poor girl who attended his schools to take home free as much as she had spun at school while listening to instructions or spiritual reading. He also gave these poor girls a free luncheon.

The Cardinal personally instructed his teachers on teaching Religion. He encouraged them when the road was rough and by word and example inspired them to persevere, reminding them of the great service they were rendering God and man by educating these young girls according to Christian principles, putting them on the way of eternal salvation. The good teacher is like a candle which lights others while consuming itself.

"If *you* do not go to heaven neither shall I"—he used to tell his teachers.

"My teachers should be like rain-clouds, refreshing every soul in this diocese.

"Before you become a canal you must be a reservoir, giving to others only from the abundance of your heart."

He expected his teachers to acquire solid virtue and personal spiritual perfection before being sent to teach others the way to Christian living. Each year he gathered all his teachers for a spiritual retreat, preached ordinarily by priests of the Society of the *Pii Operai*—Pious Workmen—who remained for a long time the spiritual guides of the Religious Teachers and of Lucy herself; the Cardinal never failed to give specific instructions during these retreats.

With such well trained teachers the school became a real temple where a new Christian generation was formed through the merit of Cardinal Barbarigo and the work of Lucy Filippini and her helpers.

Lucy Filippini and Rose Venerini shared each in her own sphere the work and the trials of a poor teacher's life here on earth; today, they both share the never-ending glory of the Saints in Heaven and the veneration decreed for them by the Church here on earth.

Lucy Filippini—much younger in years—started later towards that work and that glory, but she arrived first.[10]

[10] The Religious Teachers Filippini have only been forty-three years in America and have already given ample evidence of the spiritual vigor and apostolic zeal that animated their saintly Foundress two hundred years ago. In 1910, the Holy Father, Blessed Pius X, sent the first five Religious Teachers Filippini to America. They opened their first school for Italo-American children in Trenton, N. J. During the first years, they were beset by many difficulties like all pioneers. However, through the personal interest and the generous cooperation of the late Archbishop Thomas J. Walsh, first as Bishop of Trenton, then as Archbishop of Newark, the Sisters were soon established firmly on American soil and began to expand rapidly. In the summer of 1953 the American Province of the Religious Teachers Filippini numbers close to five hundred members, living in eighty different houses—teaching in Elementary and High Schools, Missions, Academies, etc. There are houses of the Institute in five Archdioceses and seventeen Dioceses of the Eastern United States. They also are in charge —by order of our Holy Father—of the *Domus Pacis* in Rome, Italy, an international center of Catholic Youth Organizations.

The Provincial headquarters with novitiate, house of studies, etc., are in Morristown, N. J. This is at present the center of the Institute in America. It is located on the highest and most picturesque hill of northern New Jersey, in a beautiful estate of one hundred and twenty-six acres of land. For further information write to: Rev. Mother Provincial—Religious Teachers Filippini—Villa Walsh—Morristown, New Jersey.

CHAPTER SEVEN

THE SOUL OF THE INSTITUTE.

THE truth of the old saying—"what's well begun, is half done" was manifest in the beginning of the Institute of the Religious Teachers. Conceived by the great mind and generous heart of Cardinal Barbarigo, the work received its form and permanent character from the genial mind and the heroic spirit of Lucy Filippini. The beginning, however, and the various stages of its development were made possible by both the moral and material support and the vigilance of Cardinal Barbarigo.

Heroism has sometimes been defined as the self-devotion of a genius, manifesting itself in action. No matter what the age, sex, or education, a Saint is always a genius and an heroic Christian. A genius, according to Carlyle, has an immense capacity for taking trouble. In the case of a saint like Lucy "that immense capacity" means heroic virtue, heroic patience.

There was a transcending aspiration in Lucy's life: saving souls for God! To this absorbing desire, she sacrificed everything, bodily health and life itself.

From the very beginning of the Institute, she had had to do great violence to herself in accepting the direction of the schools. She had obeyed in the darkness of faith, and that sort of obedience is the greatest sacrifice for the human spirit, acting against natural inclinations, without any advantage except that of obedience itself. Such was Abraham's obedience to the voice of God demanding the sacrifice of his only son Isaac, on whose life depended the fulfillment of God's promises. The responsibility for all the schools of the diocese which had been hurriedly established and given a rather precarious existence was a heavy burden, and Lucy had been asked to carry that burden. It was a great undertaking for whose success and stability there was no human assurance. Lucy must have had a presentiment of the bitter trials that would distress her during the last years of her life, trials caused by the position she had been asked to assume. In spite of all this Lucy obeyed the Cardinal and went to live with the other teachers in the school of Montefiascone. To show his love and interest in the Religious Teachers, the Cardinal himself designed their religious habit, according fully with the ideals of Christian modesty and humility. The habit consisted of a black serge dress, a black silk bonnet, a white scarf extending over the shoulders beneath the habit and showing at the neck, and a small silk cape. Except for a slight change introduced by Monsignor De Merode, Almoner of Pope Pius IX, the present habit of the Religious Teachers Filippini is the same as the one designed by Cardinal Barbarigo and worn by St. Lucy Filippini.

Every religious institute must have some distinctive sign, especially in religious garb and particular rules, and Cardinal Barbarigo gave the Religious Teachers a proper habit and special rules of their own. This circumstance alone would be sufficient to make him the Founder of the Religious Teachers. At first the rules themselves were not given in writing by the Cardinal but by word of mouth in his frequent instructions to the Teachers. After his death, his successor, Bishop Sebastian Bonaventura, commanded that the rules, faithfully observed by the Religious Teachers, should be put in writing and published for the benefit of future generations of Teachers. This was done by a priest of the local Seminary of Montefiascone, Canon Alexander Mazzinelli.

The rules were first published in the year 1717. There was a revision of them under Pope Clement XIII. After the publication of the new Code of Canon Law by Benedict XV, the rules were brought in conformity with the Code. In this latest revised form they were published again in 1919, with a Preface by Card. G. B. Nasalli Rocca who, as Almoner of the Pope, at that time, was their immediate superior. The latest edition bears the autographed approval of His Holiness Pope Pius XII. In this form, the rules retain the spirit of Cardinal Barbarigo and the character of St. Lucy Filippini who first and best lived those rules and gave them her own soul.

The practical test of a rule as a norm for perfection is realized when a Christian, having lived according to it is canonized by the Church. Lucy Filippini is the best proof of the sanctity of Barbarigo's rules.

The generous sacrifice made by Lucy soon proved that her spirit could endure more than her body. The more she tried to overcome her aversion and repugnance, the more bitter became the inner conflict. She was still human, as are all Saints, but she did not intend to remain so and she fought constantly against herself. In the long run, her bodily health began to fail. There was nothing alarming at first and she paid no attention to it. She carried on her duties as teacher, principal, and superior of the community. She concealed with great effort from her pupils and her spiritual daughters her real condition. Then one day her appetite failed completely, she had no strength left to carry on any longer, and she was finally forced to remain in bed and to have a doctor summoned. She suffered a widespread swelling over her body with a constant, slow fever that seemed to consume her. The forecast of the mysterious sickness was unfavorable, and Lucy remained in bed for over a year, often thinking that the same Lord who had asked for the sacrifice of her spirit was now demanding that of her body and of life itself.

Cardinal Barbarigo realized that Lucy's death would be an irreparable loss for the young Institute. Probably the whole idea of the schools would have to be abandoned, so spared no time or effort to find a remedy and a cure. At his own expenses he called the best medical doctors to take care of Lucy. He constantly inquired about her, requesting Lucy's relatives and friends to visit and comfort her. He also asked certain spiritual persons in whom she had great confidence to call frequently on her to give her any spiritual assistance she needed.

In spite of all the remedies and the extraordinary care, there seemed to be no change whatever in Lucy's condition at the end of a year. Had the Lord intended this trial as a passive mystical purgation of her soul; was it her passive dark night of the senses and the spirit? This is the extraordinary test whereby the human soul is purged and mystically remolded to fit into God's plans. It is a painful experience, but its marvelous effects last for the rest of the earthly existence.

The Lord finally remembered Lucy, for she must have thought she had been abandoned by God—a very common feeling of the passive dark night—and she began to feel a little better in body and spirit. The recovery was not very long and she felt as if she had come out of a dark tunnel into bright sunlight. It seemed like a new world and a new life she was coming back to, and she noticed too that she herself was marvelously changed.

Her attitude towards the schools had become one of love and enthusiasm. She even thought that her religious habit was beautiful, and she could not wait for the day when she could begin to teach again. That day came and still convalescent, she went to the classroom. Being still too weak to stand on her feet she sat down and, leaning her head against the wall, began to teach and to talk of the mysteries of faith with such fervor and depth as to enrapture young and old in her audience. She looked now at the little girls' souls as so many images of God committed to her care to reestablish them more and more in God's own likeness.

Fear and love of God were her main topics. God's justice, goodness, and mercy were the motives for fear and love she often explained. To these she added her favorite subject, the Passion and Death of Our Lord, as she had done from the time she was a young catechist in Tarquinia.

Order, silence, and diligent application were the basic rules of Lucy's classroom. She knew, that the children's attention cannot remain focused on one subject for a long time, so she arranged the exercises of the various grades to break the monotony and to keep the children's interest alive. Even silence was often broken by singing a sacred hymn or saying the Rosary together. One of her duties as Principal of the school was to give and explain the points of meditation for both children and adult women. On such occasions she revealed extraordinary gifts from the Holy Spirit, and showed how full her own heart was of the things she proposed to others for meditation.

After Lucy's recovery from the long sickness, she began to treasure more than ever the counsels and instructions Cardinal Barbarigo gave his teachers. These instructions were the norms and rules of the future Institute of the Religious Teachers. Im-

Lucy, the Religious Teacher

itating the example of the Blessed Virgin Mary, Lucy tried to keep all these things carefully in her heart, so that when the time came to put the rules in writing she could repeat faithfully from memory to Father Mazzinelli everything she had heard from the lips of Cardinal Barbarigo many years before.

On reading these *Instructions* today, one has the impression of hearing the venerable Cardinal himself address the first young teachers, and of Lucy years later dictating the same *Instructions* for the benefit of future generations of Religious Teachers.

"The life of our Teachers," so the rules say, "is one that is free from the restrictions of the cloister and the distractions of the world. They thus enjoy the prerogatives of both states of life without being hindered by their disadvantages. Those who are sheltered in a Cloister find less occasion for sin and greater assurance of salvation, even though they lack opportunity and merit of working directly for the salvation of souls, while those, who live in the world have a greater opportunity to practice the works of mercy, even if their salvation is exposed to greater dangers. To discover the secret of a middle course, that of living in the world without being exposed to all its dangers and withdrawing from it without losing the merit of helping our neighbor with sound instruction and good example, is to find a third state of life, wherein Teachers harmonize the duties of the religious life with those of the secular life. Separating whatever is useful and perfect in those two conditions of life from what is less advantageous for their souls, they are willingly to accept the labors and hardships of those states. Deprived of worldly satisfactions, they must live like solitaries. On the other hand renouncing the peace and repose of solitaries, they are to dedicate themselves to works of charity.

"Nor is this sort of life a new one in the Church. This was the mode of life followed by the Christian Virgins of the early centuries, when there were neither Convents nor Monasteries. The chaste spouses of the Lord lived in the midst of the world. Their own virtue and the respect with which they were surrounded was sufficient protection for their innocence. Wisely dividing their time between contemplation, divine worship, and works of charity with social assistance, they were neither idle in their solitude nor distracted in their charitable assistance."[1]

Sound teaching and good example are greatly needed in the world at all times. The main mission of the Religious Teachers is to teach by word and example, to be in the world but not of it. The example of early Christians offers the purest norm of practical Christianity, the norm Cardinal Barbarigo offered to his teachers.

In early Christian centuries, the unknown author of the *Epistle to Diognetus* wrote: "Just as the soul dwells in the body, yet is not of the body; thus the Christians dwell in the world, yet are not of the world. . . . The soul when poorly provided with food and drink, becomes better; in like manner the Christians though persecuted increase in number daily."[2]

Our present generation, realizing the efficiency and the timeliness of such secular institutes, has acknowledged the practical and far-seeing minds of Cardinal Barbarigo and Lucy Filippini.

"With this Institute—The Religious Teachers—we do not pretend to start a new Religious Order nor to bind our Teachers with any religious vows. There is no doubt, however, that those called to this kind of work must lead a life entirely different

---

[1] A. MAZZINELLI. *Istruzione per regolamento delle Scuole.* Pag. 13 f.
[2] *Epistle to Diognetus,* VI.

from the life of the common man or woman. Therefore, it is not enough that they live according to the Commandments, they must, in addition, follow the evangelical counsels, not obliged thereto by vows but by the desire of Christian perfection. They would fail in the profession of their state if, satisfied with what is of precept, they did not apply themselves to the study and the practice of evangelical perfection."[3]

The Institute has no religious vows but makes a solemn promise to keep the evangelical counsels of Poverty, Chastity, and Obedience. This promise is equivalent to a private vow. Religious vows are public and have canonical effects not connected with private vows.[4] The Institute belongs in the category of Societies of Common Life (Code of Canon Law, Book II, Title XVII, Canons 673-681). In the preamble to his Constitution *Provida Mater Ecclesia,* of February 2, 1947, Pope Pius XII said that these Societies have been granted by the Church "a full measure of equality with the canonical state of perfection." For this reason people call them *Sisters* even though such title is not found in any of the official documents concerning them. In the latest edition of their Rules they are called simply *Maestre*—Teachers. The Religious Teachers do not assume a religious name, retaining their own baptismal and family name for life, nor do they cut their hair as most religious women do. All this is in keeping with the spirit of St. Lucy Filippini and with the constant tradition of the Institute. Lucy Filippini is never called Sister or Mother by her biographers but simply *La Signora Lucia*—Lady Lucy.

Imbued with the spirit of St. Francis of Assisi, Lucy gladly complied with the Cardinal's wish to retain the civil name and

---

[3] A. MAZZINELLI, op. cit., page 43 f.
[4] *The Code of Canon Law,* canon 673.

the title, Maestra. *Sisters* and *Mothers* savor too much of the Cloister and the Cardinal did not want such an impression left in the mind of his *Maestre*. To St. Francis of Assisi, the title Sister, given to religious women, implied too much familiarity and he disapproved of it. He did not like to hear people call St. Clare and her nuns *Sorores*—Sisters, and he approached his Cardinal Protector with the request that they be called instead *Dominae*—Ladies. If he heard nuns called *Sisters,* he was troubled and said: "The Lord has delivered us from wives, and now the devil has given us sisters."[5]

Lucy's apostolate of Christian education was not restricted to the classroom and the school hours. Then she could watch the pupils herself or through some of her teachers. Her interest in their good behavior extended to all times and places even outside the school. She therefore often inquired from parents and relatives about the conduct of the girls when they were not at school. If faults and misbehavior were reported, she earnestly corrected and warned the girls; and if the gravity of the fault committed demanded, she punished them.

Often Lucy did not have to ask for information about her pupils. Through some charismatic gift of reading the secrets of conscience, she seemed to know everything they had done when away from school. The girls became so convinced of this that they dared not appear before her when their conscience reproached them with some fault.

After the girls left the schools and had reached a marriageable age, Lucy expected them to return to school for a retreat of eight full days a short time before a wedding. During this retreat they were instructed about the special duties of Christian

[5] N. DE ROBECK. *St. Clare of Assisi.* Pag. 44.

wives and mothers, on the sanctity of Christian marriage, and how to approach this Sacrament in the state of grace. Cardinal Barbarigo with his customary charity gave each poor girl the necessary marriage dowry on condition that they had made the retreat mentioned, presenting a certificate signed by Lucy Filippini to prove it.

Reform and sanctification of human society begin with marriage, the parents, and the children. Such was Barbarigo's plan of reform and Lucy was commissioned to carry it out. She did this for nearly forty years of her life, her genius of devotion and her heroism manifesting itself in action. She brought light where there had been darkness, peace where strife and war had ruled. Child of God that she was, she became a peacemaker in every town she visited. Whenever the Cardinal heard of any breach of concord between families or individuals, he summoned Lucy and said:

"Look, my child, we have done so much and we have accomplished so little. People still quarrel, wrangle, and offend God!

"Go, Lucy, bring peace and reconcile the quarreling parties!"

Lucy went immediately. She first spoke to each side, touching their hearts and bringing tears to their eyes. She then brought them together, and in her presence they renewed their friendship after expressing sorrow for whatever had caused them to quarrel.

A sinner can be defined as one who has an immense capacity for making trouble for the love of self. A saint—the genius— as one who has an immense capacity for taking trouble for the love of God and neighbor. Lucy was such a saint and such a genius.

CHAPTER EIGHT

MOLDING THE SPIRIT.

IF the profession of a teacher, molding the mind of children, has been compared to sculpture and painting and adjudged superior to both those noble arts, what must be the worth and the excellence of one who molds and forms both the mind and the heart of future teachers?

Lucy Filippini acted both as school teacher for children and as instructor of pedagogy for future teachers. She was, in addition, the Mistress of novices and the Superior of the Institute. All these duties and responsibilities were actually joined in her heart in one sublime feeling and name, Mother. She was the spiritual Mother of all the members of her Institute. As a mother she embraced them all with pure and tender love. Young girls whose hearts were aching on leaving home and a mother's affection found even greater and purer maternal care and affection on entering Lucy's community.

As Lucy had become "a pattern to the flock from the heart"[1] both as a religious and as a teacher, her instructions to novices and future teachers had all the conquering and convincing power of good example and long experience. She wanted her young teachers at her side when she went through various school

[1] I Pet. 5:3.

exercises with the children or when she explained prayer and meditation to adult women.

School girls who did not intend to become teachers were instructed in reading, in Catechism, in handicraft for girls, but not in writing. Writing was a teacher's privilege, in those days, at least among the girls of the poor class. This restriction resulted from a widespread abuse, the writing of secret love letters to boys, a disorder much decried in that district in those days.

Lucy watched over her young teachers very carefully at all times, intent on freeing them of worldly ideas and sensual inclinations, transforming them slowly into real apostles of Christ. The words of St. Paul to the Colossians, to "walk worthy of God, in all things pleasing," must have been frequently in her mouth. Knowing that the purpose of a virtuous life is assimilation to the divine model, she daily presented the example of our Divine Savior to them in meditation.

Lucy's keen discernment in detecting the aptitude and the good intention of the candidates prevented her from clothing with the religious habit those who lacked the qualities of a true vocation. Without telling anyone the motive, she quietly dismissed the unfit and those with no vocation from the community before the time for the reception arrived.

Once the candidates had received the habit, Lucy expected them to lead a new life both interiorly and exteriorly, to be an inspiration and an example to women living in the world. Above all things they were to be firmly convinced of their vocation and to be impressed deeply with the importance of their mission.

"Ah, sisters—she would say—how great an office has the good Lord entrusted us poor little women!"

The education of youth was an apostolate for Lucy, and her teachers were trained as future apostles.

Prayer was the foundation of all spiritual perfection in the eyes of Lucy Filippini, the universal means of salvation for all. It was enough for her to see a postulant had no inclination for prayer to disqualify her as a Religious Teacher. More by her own example did Lucy instruct her Religious Teachers to pray than by word.

"The prayer of Lady Lucy—reported her spiritual daughters after her death—was continual, accompanied always by the sweetest tears. In the morning, she spent several hours in mental and vocal prayer, weeping like another Magdalen at the feet of our Lord, so much so that her companions often told her jokingly that she never stopped chanting Jeremias' *Lamentations*. No matter what business or work she was engaged in, her mouth was never closed to prayer nor did her tongue ever stop from praising God. When the meditation was on the subject of the Passion of Jesus our Savior, she had to go to the upper rooms of the house to give free expression to her feelings of sorrow and compassion with an abundance of tears."[2]

So much weeping and tears did not depress the community. Her constant prayer brought a feeling of the presence of God and became the source of ineffable spiritual joy which was reflected from her on all the members of her community, turning their humble dwelling into a place of real joy and peace.

"From her continual prayer came a constant presence of God, and from this that interior exultation and spiritual joy wherein she was seen to be happy and rejoicing always. She was heard singing while rising in the morning and on retiring at night, and many hours were spent in spiritual exultation, and so time

[2] F. DI SIMONE. *Lucia Filippini.* Pag. 114 f.

went by very quickly. Her days were like moments, and we who lived with her felt we were living in the company of a soul from the land of the Blessed, enjoying here on earth the peace and the consolation of Heaven."[3]

This precious testimony of Lucy's pupils and associates is an eloquent proof of her sanctity and of the enduring influence her saintly life had on the Institute from the beginning.

"Work and Pray!" was St. Benedict's basic rule for his monks. Lucy applied that rule to herself and to her Religious Teachers. She would tolerate no idleness in her community. Her Teachers were always engaged in some useful work or devout exercise, not only in order to avoid becoming a plaything of the devil through idleness, but also to learn how to earn their own bread.

"Sisters, not knowing what the future has in store for us, I want all my teachers to learn how to work for their livelihood."

Mortification was another basic virtue in her formation of novices. The life of a teacher is not a life of comfort but one of constant self-denial. He who loves Christ loves his cross without which no one can truly follow him. The daily cross of every Christian consists of a number of interior and exterior vexations resulting from our duties, our nature, and our environment.

Lucy was very successful with her lessons on mortification, and it soon became apparent that her disciples needed to be restrained rather than to be urged on in this respect. Of their own accord they did many things that were both painful and repulsive in order to mortify themselves. Some of them made heavy wooden crosses which they carried on their shoulders through the house while saying their prayers. Others climbed

[3] F. DI SIMONE, op. cit., page 115.

the stairs on their knees in spirit of penance, and they all did many other things that our present generation may regard as offensive.

While approving the moderate use of austerities and exterior mortifications, Lucy insisted particularly on the mortification of the will, in which self-denial really consists. Self-love can coexist with austerities, and it may be found hiding behind exterior mortifications, especially those of a showy nature. Interior mortification is a self-sacrifice known to God alone; only a prompt and perfect obedience can suggest its existence. In order to reach deep into the realm of self-love, Lucy studied each teacher in order to command her to do something that was exactly opposed to her inclination.

The spirit of the Saints counts more than the things they did. What they did, at times, was rather odd and strange. It would be a mistake to imitate them materially by repeating what they did without possessing their spirit. Lucy had the spirit of the great apostle of Rome, St. Philip Neri, and thus she, at times, imitated him in imposing strange and queer penances on her disciples.

Lucy and her community were at table one day, and as was customary, one of the Teachers was reading from a spiritual book. She had just read how St. Philip Neri used to check the pride and self-love of his disciples by commanding them to do things that would make them appear ridiculous and contemptible in the eyes of the world, when Lucy had an inspiration. She wanted to know how her disciples would react to a similar test of their virtue. She interrupted the meal, stopping the reader.

"Come here, all of you!" she said. "I want to cut your eyebrows."

Without hesitation all the members of the community got up from the table and kneeled around Lucy with an eagerness which clearly indicated how well established they were in the virtue of obedience and in mortification. Lucy then clipped just a little from each one's eyebrows without disfiguring them.

As was to be expected, the devil's advocate, during Lucy's Process of Beatification, did not miss this particular incident. He used it as an objection against Lucy's virtue, calling this action a sign of a nervous and hot-headed character: *cerebrosae indolis*.[4] It was explained, however, that both her action, her intention and the salutary effects were in keeping with virtue.

Modesty in dress and gait was another virtue insisted upon by the Saintly Teacher.

"Our Teachers should despise this world. God has placed us in this state of life in order that we may give a good example to the women who live in the world. What will these poor ladies think if they see a Religious Teacher strutting around gaudily dressed?"

Inspired by the example of St. Francis and St. Clare of Assisi, Lucy loved poverty in dress, food, lodging, and everything else in this life. The shabbiest and most threadbare dress in the house was hers. She had no change of dress or underwear. Many times her Teachers had to force her to accept another dress or another shirt when what she was wearing could no longer be repaired. She accepted such things as a beggar from a benefactor.

Both prayer and work demand solitude and recollection. He who loves to talk always with men shows that he converses but little with God, said St. Alphonsus Liguori. A school teacher is exposed to the danger of losing interior recollection because

---

[4] Summarium, etc. No. 53.

of school activities and unavoidable social contact with seculars. St. Lucy Filippini was well aware of this danger and she never ceased warning her young teachers of it, instructing them how to remain always united with God in spirit amid crowded classrooms or distracting social activities. In order to preserve the sprit of recollection and the love of solitude in her Religious Teachers, she did not favor visits with relatives, except in case of sickness or when charity and the greater glory of God demanded it, saying:

"At home with relatives one of us never gains, she only loses." St. Francis of Assisi's saying was often quoted by her: "He who seeks solitude escapes three dangers: those of sight, hearing, and evil speaking."

No matter how enlightened Lucy's direction of her Teachers might have been, she knew that only a Priest, as minister of God and dispenser of His mysteries, is the proper spiritual guide of souls. However, the experience of Saints and her own in this matter had taught her to be extremely careful in the choice of a spiritual Director for her Teachers. Sanctity of life, sound theological doctrine and prudence are the three necessary qualities for a good spiritual director. Should one of those qualities be missing, there is serious danger. In her own practical way, Lucy understood that such qualities are more likely to be found in elderly Priests than in younger ones. Experience in spiritual matters synthesizes these three qualities, and such experience is acquired only with age. In addition, the danger of spiritual friendships is more remote when the Director is old. Lucy restricted all the dealings with the spiritual Director to the Confessional and she tolerated no infractions to this rule.

She had arrived in a town one day, for the customary visit of one of the schools, and the spiritual Director of the community

hearing of her arrival made a call to pay his respect to Lucy. As
all the Teachers gathered around Lucy and the Director, the
latter took a snuffbox out of his pocket for his habitual snuff of
tobacco. Immediately one of the Religious Teachers reached out
to take a pinch of snuff from the Director's open box. Lucy
looked at the offender with grief and, immediately, gave her
a good lesson, saying that Teachers should never take liberties
with their Director.

Lucy's spiritual Director, or Extraordinary Confessor, was
Cardinal Barbarigo himself. He acted in this capacity for all the
Teachers of the school Montefiascone. For other schools, the
Fathers of the Society of the *Pii Operai* acted as Confessors and
Directors.

One of the duties Lucy had as Superior and Superintendent
of the schools was a periodical visitation of them, done ordinarily twice a year. Accompanied by one of her associates, she left
Montefiascone to visit one or more schools at a time, according
to their distance. The conditions of the roads and the precarious
means of transportation at her disposal afforded constant opportunity for penance and mortification during the trips. The two
women often walked for miles when no other means were
available, and often reached their destination completely exhausted. At times they were lost on the road and wandered for
hours through forests and swamps arriving with torn dresses,
their faces and hands scratched by briars. Lucy's arrival was
always greeted with joy by her Teachers who found encouragement and inspiration in the presence of their Mother. Lucy always had a ready solution to their problems; she revived fallen
spirits with her words full of light and comfort, and there were
no financial problems in those schools as long as Cardinal Barbarigo was living.

The pious Cardinal supplied yearly to each community of two or three teachers the following: thirty bushels of wheat, twelve barrels of wine, fifty pounds of cheese, twelve gallons of olive oil, eighteen gold dollars in money, and two pairs of shoes for each Teacher. Every two years, each received a new habit of black serge and a new silk bonnet.

Up to the end of his life, the Cardinal spent himself and all he possessed for his beloved Teachers and their schools. He went so far as to contract heavy debts for their sake. To some of his advisers who tried to suggest moderation in his expenditures he replied:

"It is a shame for a businessman to die impoverished and indebted, but is honorable for a Bishop to die without his breeches. The Bishop who on his death leaves a large amount of money is not worthy to be buried in sacred ground."

Lucy was appointed as the Cardinal's secret almoner for Montefiascone. Food was never to be refused to the poor knocking at their door.

The example of Christian charity of these two saintly souls was a major factor in the reform of the diocese. It also set an example for the new Institute of Religious Teachers, forming and molding them in the school of charity, which is the school of Christ Himself.

CHAPTER NINE

TRIALS AT ST. CLARE'S CONVENT.

DURING the last year of his Pontificate, Pope Innocent XII had proclaimed a great Jubilee for the coming year 1700. Pilgrims in great numbers soon started on their journey towards the Eternal City in order to gain the Indulgences connected with the Holy Year, visiting the tombs of the Princes of the Apostles and other major Basilicas of Rome.

The city of Montefiascone, on the main highway leading straight to Rome from the cities of Siena, Florence, Bologna, and other northern towns and states, was the last overnight stop in going to and the first in returning from Rome. Here the pilgrims spent the night at the Hospice before proceeding on their trip.

Hospitality was still a work of Christian charity in those days. Hospices placed at a convenient distance along the highways were the real homes of hospitality and workshops of charity. The capacity of the Hospice of Montefiascone was adequate enough for the average crowd of pilgrims going and coming from Rome ordinarily, but it was absolutely inadequate to accommodate the larger crowds stopping there during a Holy Year. Cardinal Barbarigo placed a large section of his episcopal palace at the disposal of the Holy Year's pilgrims. Lucy offered practically the entire Pennoni house, in which she stayed with her spiritual daughters, to accommodate women of the pilgrimages, and the men stayed at the episcopal palace or other private homes.

There was a kind of friendly rivalry between the saintly Cardinal and Lucy during that Holy Year in offering hospitality and all possible service and attention to the pilgrims. One of the Cardinal's chaplains received the pilgrims and gave them the necessary instructions upon their arrival. When all were assembled the Cardinal himself came down to greet and to give them a short instruction on some point of Christian Doctrine. This done, the Cardinal washed the feet of thirteen of the men, while other pious persons did the same for the rest of the pilgrims. After the washing of the feet, he invited all the pilgrims to the upper floor where tables were set for supper. The Cardinal personally served at table while one of his priests read from a pious book for the edification of the guests. All this was done with such love and reverence that the pilgrims felt restored both in body and spirit, being deeply edified by such virtue.

The Cardinal's charity on this occasion was equalled by that of Lucy who with no less fervor and generosity did the same for the women pilgrims. She received them all with great cordiality, washed their feet, and served them at table with such love and respect as to show clearly that in the person of those pilgrims she honored and served our Blessed Lord himself. In addition, Lucy extended her service and hospitality to the priests who accompanied the pilgrims. These were housed in the Hospice proper which stood across the street from Lucy's headquarters. An old maid servant was in charge of the Hospice, but Lucy went there daily to help her with her work, sweeping and cleaning the rooms, and doing other menial duties.

Before the Holy Year came to a close, Pope Innocent XII

died and Cardinal Barbarigo was forced to go to Rome to the Conclave for the election of a new Pontiff. During his absence, the work of charity and hospitality continued unabated under Lucy's care and supervision.

The abundant graces connected with this work were to strengthen Lucy's soul for a series of trials at the Convent of St. Clare. The relaxed discipline and the resulting financial difficulties of the *Monachelle* of St. Clare's Convent had been of no little concern to the Cardinal ever since his arrival at Montefiascone. He had tried various ways to bring the "Little Nuns" back to their former religious spirit and discipline but without success. They had been as much a cause of pain to him as Lucy and her Teachers had been of joy and satisfaction.

The *Monachelle* had outlived their usefulness in the diocese. Very reluctant to suppress their community, the Cardinal decided to bring about a radical change in their Convent. The building was to serve as Lucy's Motherhouse for her Religious Teachers. There would be a novitiate for new teachers, a home for Religious Teachers who needed to be retired, and finally an additional school for girls, because the existing one was no longer sufficient for the town of Montefiascone. The *Monachelle* had to fall in line and conform to the new arrangement. Nobody thought that they would comply peacefully to any change in their mode of living, but Divine Providence afforded the opportunity for the realization of the new plan.

The Mother Superior of the *Monachelle,* Sister Clare F. Mereanzi of Bagnorea, requested the Cardinal through her own Confessor, the Prior of the Augustinians, to grant her permission to leave her Convent and to join Lucy Filippini's community, because she was unable to bear the poverty and the wretched conditions of St. Clare's Convent any longer. The

Cardinal seized this opportunity for presenting his plan to the *Monachelle*. He assured them that they could continue to live in their Convent and that their living conditions would be improved and that he would provide for them for the rest of their lives. Their Convent, however, was to be converted into a Motherhouse for the Religious Teachers with a school for girls. Lucy Filippini would be the Superior of the house and the *Monachelle* themselves would become part of her community wearing the same habit and keeping the rules he would give them. This plan was given in writing to the Augustinian Prior with the order to read and explain it to the *Monachelle* who readily accepted it.

On October 6, 1704, the Cardinal went to St. Clare's Convent accompanied by two priests in order to explain his plan to the assembled community.

"If you are disposed to join the Religious Teachers, assisting them in their apostolate with your prayers and mortifications, and if you accept and keep the rules that we give to the community, we will support you and provide for all your needs, so that you may serve the Lord in peace and tranquillity of mind."

All the Sisters, except one, expressed their willingness to comply with the Cardinal's wishes. The dissenting one, Sister Mary Angela Piacentini, joined the Benedictine Nuns of Tarquinia with full approval of Cardinal Barbarigo.

Having thus obtained the *Monachelle's* consent, the Cardinal presented his plan to Lucy Filippini. They decided to inaugurate the new community with the greatest solemnity possible. All the Religious Teachers of the Institute were summoned to Montefiascone and assembled in St. Clare's Convent. A spiritual retreat was made by all the assembled Teachers and the *Monachelle,* beginning on October 7, and closing on the Feast of St. Teresa, October 15. On this day the Cardinal himself celebrated the Holy Sacrifice of the Mass in the Church of St. Clare and gave Holy Communion to all those who had made the retreat. After Mass he blessed the black habits of the Religious Teachers and gave them to the *Monachelle,* to wear in place of their former grey religious habit. The Cardinal made an exception for one of the *Monachelle* who begged him to be allowed to continue to wear her old habit, but she too asked for the new habit the following day and received it. With the reception of the new habit the Cardinal officially converted the old Convent of St. Clare into a house for Religious Teachers, transferring to it all the debts and revenues of the former Convent and promising new sources of income for their support. The new name of the Convent was: *Casa Pia delle Maestre Pie* —Religious House of the Religious Teachers. Both the name and the new arrangement of the community had a very short life. The Cardinal restored and enlarged the old building adapting it to its new purpose. He spent more than a thousand gold-dollars on such work during the first year alone.

Lucy Filippini's return to the former Convent of St. Clare, no longer as a pupil and a subject but as a superior and a teacher, was not to be a happy and lasting one. She obeyed the Cardinal and did everything on her part to carry out his plan. Her virtue and tact would have been sufficient for the realization of the new plan. Another element, however, was needed for complete success, the good will and humility of the former *Monachelle.* It soon became evident that this second element did not exist.

Lucy entered upon her new position with profound humility and great charity, acting more like a servant than the superior of the mixed community. The Feast of St. Teresa of Avila which marked the opening of the new House reminded her of

circumstances somewhat like those that had confronted the seraphic virgin of Avila soon after the beginning of her reform of
the Carmel. To prevent the development of her reform, she
had been appointed prioress of the Convent of Avila which
she had left in order to begin her reform. The nuns of that
Convent resented her "adventure," regarding it as an aspersion
on their religious spirit. They received her with manifest hos-
tility. The Saint had the gracious idea of putting a statue of our
Blessed Lady in the place ordinarily occupied by the prioress
with the keys of the Convent hanging from Our Lady's arm,
and this unexpected attitude softened the hearts of most of her
subjects. Lucy followed a similar course with the former *Monachelle* but not with equal success. While her own spiritual
daughters surrounded her with their customary affection and
promptly obeyed her, the new members of the community—the
Monachelle—who had changed their habit but not their habits,
resented her authority and opposed her constantly.

Jealousy entered the heart of the former superior, the same
Sister Clare F. Mereanzi of Bagnorea who had asked to be received in Lucy's community. She could not accept the fact that
young Lucy, their former pupil, enjoyed the full confidence of
the Cardinal and was succeeding where she had failed. She
expressed her resentment by indulging in a destructive criticism
of the new superior among her former associates. Lucy was
finally forced to call her to order, in all charity and humility, but
Sister Clare called such corrections a veritable persecution, com-
plaining about Lucy even to outsiders. She probably hoped to
disconcert Lucy and break her morale, and so force her to resign.
Lucy continued to hold her position with dignity and firmness,
pained but not disturbed by the campaign of dislike. Sister
Clare Mereanzi finally decided to run away from the Convent in

a way—she thought—that would reflect on Lucy's administration of the community. Eluding the vigilance of the house one evening, she slipped out by a back door of the Convent and returned to her home town. Rebellion against authority is somewhat contagious and rebels usually find willing imitators. Soon other *Monachelle* threatened to leave the Convent unless Lucy stopped demanding a regular observance of the rule. Lucy was not one to be intimidated or to compromise with religious unworthy of the name. She stuck firmly to the ideals of reform set down by the Cardinal. A crisis was forming. Two other former religious ran away and went home. The remaining *Monachelle* were ready to follow their example but the fear of having to go hungry if they left the Convent prevented them from running away. Their conduct in the Convent became a scandal to the whole town, disturbing the peace of the house and inciting others to rebellion.

Cardinal Barbarigo was absent from Montefiascone while the storm raged but poor Lucy was in the midst of it. She saw the futility of any attempt at reforming the *Monachelle*. She had to acknowledge that the Cardinal's plan had failed. She remembered the words of our Savior about the salt that has lost its savor. It is not good for any other purpose and should be cast out. The *Monacelle* had long ago lost their religious spirit. They were really like the salt that had lost its savor; they should have been suppressed.

Alone, without the comforting and reassuring presence of the Cardinal and without one hour of peace, Lucy wrote a letter to Cardinal Barbarigo requesting him to relieve her of her present position that she might give all her attention to the schools which would undoubtedly suffer greatly if the present trying circumstances lasted much longer. The Cardinal found

Lucy's decision very sensible and granted her request, asking her, however, to wait until his return before making any changes.

For nearly three years Lucy felt the pangs of remorse and she grieved and wept bitterly over this fault—if fault it was—for she thought that the Cardinal had granted her request only to please her. She regarded her action as a weakness, but quitting under such circumstances was an act of virtue and not a weakness. By doing so she prevented greater evils to her Institute. The troublesome *Monachelle* were the real weaklings, because they did not have the moral courage to leave, nor sufficient grace and good will to reform their conduct.

The other portion of the community, the Religious Teachers and the new school, could not thrive in an atmosphere of discord and rebellion created by the incorrigible *Monachelle,* who had little in common with Lucy's spiritual daughters except the new habit. The Cardinal had to look for another solution of the thorny problem of the *Monachelle.* While still in Rome, he met a pious priest, Don Biagio Morani, of the collegiate church of St. Marc. He was the spiritual director of a number of souls, one of whom was the Roman, Miss Catherine Comaschi, thirty-nine years old, who had tried in vain to enter the Convent of St. Restituta in Narni. Under Don Morani's direction, she had made considerable progress in the ways of Christian perfection. Don Morani proposed her to the Cardinal as a worthy successor to Lucy in the Convent of St. Clare. Catherine Comaschi was wise enough to realize that a superior of a religious community must have been a novice and a religious subject for some time, and she had no experience of community life. She refused for some time, but finally consented to assume the direction of the mixed community. She arrived in Montefiascone on February 4, 1705. On the following day she was installed as superior by the Cardinal who exhorted the remaining *Monachelle* and the young Teachers to obey her. Some of the *Monachelle,* true to their traditions, left the community rather than obey the new superior.

Freed of her office, Lucy returned to her former headquarters, the school on St. Margaret's square in Montefiascone, resuming the direction of her Teachers and schools. A few of her young Teachers remained at St. Clare's house under the direction of the new superior, Sister Catherine Comaschi.

The Cardinal had hoped that with a new superior peace and harmony would be established at St. Clare's Convent, but the hope proved to be an illusion. The new superior, with no experience, was accustomed to an unyielding and severe form of discipline and piety. From the first days of her regime, she imposed community life and a multitude of religious practices on everybody, both Teachers and *Monachelle.* The Teachers soon found themselves handicapped in their school work by these new exercises. They complained to Lucy because the welfare of the schools and the Teachers still remained her concern. She was pained to hear this and brought the complaint to the attention of the new superior with no result. Lucy advised patience and obedience, telling the Teachers in the mean time to remain at St. Clare's Convent until Cardinal Barbarigo returned from Tarquinia where he was staying at the time.

Soon after her installation Sister Catherine Comaschi had asked the Cardinal to allow a friend of hers, a certain Catherine Ridolfi of Castel Gandolfo to come and help her. She thought that her position would be strengthened if her friend joined the community.

Towards the end of March of that year Catherine Ridolfi arrived at St. Clare's Convent in company with their common friend Miss Costanza Costanzi of Rome. The Cardinal felt that the presence of Don Morani would be of great help both to the new superior and her community. He begged him to transfer from Rome to Montefiascone for the benefit of his former penitents and the community. Don Morani arrived on the 14th of May and took lodging at the local Hospice near Lucy's school.

In spite of solid spirituality, Don Morani lacked the practical piety needed in the apostolate of the schools and in Catholic action. His ideal was to change every member of the mixed community of St. Clare into a contemplative, free of every outside engagement of the active life. He therefore misunderstood Lucy Filippini, characterizing her as "a person averse to living in community either because she loved her own tranquillity of mind or had tired of the intrigues and the confusion existing in that community." As a spiritual director he seems to have lacked the necessary discretion and sound judgment, as the mistaken appraisal of Lucy's spirit witnesses.

With the arrival of these new elements the Cardinal decided to set up an entirely new form of religious community at St. Clare's Convent. Theoretically the new project was harmonious and inspiring, but in practice it was soon revealed as inefficient and unworkable because of the factor called "human element." The purpose of the new project was to harmonize the two separate currents in the community, the active life of the schools of the Religious Teachers with the contemplative life of the *Monachelle* and the new comers, Sister Comaschi and her friends.

In the same Convent of St. Clare therefore, there was to be a *Congregation of the Divine Love* and a *Home of the Heavenly Spouse*. The members of the Congregation, thirteen in number, were to be called *The Preelect,* those of the Home of equal number, were to be *The Elect.* The *Preelect* were the contemplatives of the community, with duties similar to those of cloistered nuns, the chanting of the Divine Office, and a multitude of other spiritual exercises. The *Elect* were exempt from the Divine Office, and except for a few religious practices, their time was to be devoted to school work. The Cardinal in his project had given equal active and passive voice to both branches of the community, but Don Morani and the new Superior managed to have the *Elect,* the Religious Teachers, declared ineligible for such offices of the community as superior, assistant superior, secretary, mistress of novices, mistress of postulants, etc. There were in addition four lay sisters bringing the number of the entire community to thirty. The Cardinal entrusted Don Morani with the execution of his plan.

It had been the Cardinal's desire that both Lucy and her local Religious Teachers freely join the *Home of the Heavenly Spouse,* in quality of *Elect.* Lucy immediately sensed the danger for the life of her schools and declined to join. It was too evident that the new superior with the help of Don Morani would have eventually smothered all school activity absorbing the Teachers into their own orbit. Only two Religious Teachers joined the *Congregation of the Divine Love,* as *Preelect.* Lucy's example was followed by all the other Religious Teachers who decided not to be entangled in new experiments.

For the first time, a real difference of opinion between Lucy Filippini and Cardinal Barbarigo appeared. The Cardinal was deeply grieved by Lucy's attitude on this occasion. He must have disclosed his feelings to some of his friends for people soon began to say publicly that Lucy had incurred the Cardinal's disfavor.

On hearing such rumors Lucy realized that her position as superintendent of schools and superior of all Religious Teachers had been undermined. She decided to quietly relinquish her double office. She therefore applied to Father Martinelli, S.J. and to Rose Venerini for permission to join their schools in Viterbo. She remembered well Rose Venerini's uncompromising attitude with regard to the activity of a teacher, and she fully agreed with her on this point. The teacher had to be free of any other duty, even those of a Third Order, to dedicate her whole self to the school. No other engagement, no interference from any quarter was to be tolerated. Lucy had sacrificed her inclinations for a contemplative life to please the Cardinal, and to dedicate herself to the schools; now others were trying to nullify her work in favor of some would-be contemplatives. This, no doubt, was one of Lucy's darkest hours. She was about to sever the sacred and friendly relations with the saintly Cardinal and her spiritual daughters, and she must have felt the bitter agony of the step she was taking.

When the Cardinal heard the sinister rumors that Lucy had incurred his disfavor, he lost no time in giving a public and solemn demonstration of his unchanged esteem and affection for her. He invited her to his palace one day with the intention of proving how groundless and false the rumors were.

"Ask for any favor you want, my daughter, and it shall be granted." Deeply moved, Lucy replied:

"This one favor do I ask of Your Eminence: please, help me to bring souls to God!"

The Cardinal was both edified and moved by such a request. He had just heard the cry of Lucy's soul, the sublime expression of her most ardent desire in life. She knew by experience that the school offers an excellent opportunity for bringing souls to God. She wanted to save the schools at all cost, and she succeeded.

Lucy remained at her post as superior and superintendent of schools, forgetting about her application to Rose Venerini. From that day she became the savior of her schools and of her Institute. Thus, once again, she became the foundress of the Religious Teachers Filippini.

Lucy's action with regard to the new community of St. Clare's Convent was fully justified by later events. Soon after the death of Cardinal Barbarigo, Don Morani proceeded to change over the *Congregation of the Divine Love* and to suppress the *Home of the Heavenly Spouse,* to which the Religious Teachers should have belonged, just as Lucy Filippini had foreseen. Some time later, solemn religious vows and Papal enclosure were introduced at St. Clare's Convent, and thus the transformation was complete.

CHAPTER TEN

THE CARDINAL GOES TO HIS REWARD.

THE religious and moral reform of the diocese of Montefiascone and Corneto Tarquinia had become an accomplished fact and a cause of great satisfaction for Cardinal Barbarigo. Lucy and her Religious Teachers were responsible in a high degree for the successful results of his efforts. To the end of his life, the Cardinal worked relentlessly in the care and solicitude for all his churches. He had never failed to make the annual visitation of the entire diocese. Imitating the example of our Divine Savior on such occasions, the Cardinal used to send Lucy and one of her companions into every town and hamlet he was about to visit. Lucy prepared the people of the towns for the pastoral visitation by giving spiritual exercises to the women of the place. She also inquired about existing abuses and disorders which she then related to the Cardinal that he might correct them on his arrival.

The last of these pastoral visits was made to the towns of Marta, Valentano, Latera, Gradoli, San Lorenzo, Celleno, and Grotte di Castro. During the visitation in the last named town the Cardinal felt the first symptoms of the infirmity which was to bring him to his grave in less than a week.

Returning to Montefiascone on the vigil of Pentecost, May 22, 1706, he assisted in the choir of his Cathedral church at First Vespers of the Feast that afternoon. The following morning, Pentecost Sunday, unmindful of a high fever and an extremely weakened condition, he recited the canonical hours of the Divine Office on his knees, as was his custom, and then went to the Cathedral to officiate at the Pontifical High Mass and to preach to his flock.

This was the last sacred function of Cardinal Barbarigo, his last Mass and last sermon. When he blessed his people at the end of the Pontifical Mass, he felt that his tired hand would never be raised again to implore God's blessings over his flock.

Lucy who was present in the Cathedral that morning had noticed the pain and the exhaustion of every gesture and word of her beloved spiritual father, forebodings of an imminent tragedy for the people of the diocese and especially for herself. She must have wept secretly when receiving that last blessing from her spiritual guide and protector. She felt that the good Lord was calling His faithful laborer home to his reward. The evening of his life had come and the shadows were falling. The luminous light that had guided her steps for so many years was about to fade away forever.

Reentering his episcopal palace after the Pontifical Mass in a state of complete exhaustion, the saintly Cardinal could no longer conceal his real condition. He was put to bed—a very sick man.

The following day, feeling that his end was fast approaching, he ordered that six hundred Holy Masses be said for the repose of his soul in each of the six major churches of the city. His confessor, Don Biagio Morani, was summoned and the Cardinal made a general confession of his entire life with many tears and other signs of real sorrow. From that moment, abandoning all thoughts of the life and the earth he was leaving, he prepared himself with humble and fervent prayers to meet his Creator.

Early on May 26, he received Extreme Unction and after a painful agony he expired. It was about 10:30 of the morning of May 26, the Feast of St. Philip Neri, a Saint the deceased Cardinal had honored in a special manner all his life.

"Yes, says the Spirit, let them rest from their labors, for their works follow them." These words of the Apocalypse expressed the prayer and the general belief of all those present in the Cathedral as the Introit of the funeral Mass was read the day Cardinal Barbarigo's mortal remains were laid to rest.

The death of the Cardinal was a great loss not only to the diocese of Montefiascone but in a sense to the whole Church. In a public Consistory, Pope Clement XI expressed his sorrow at such a loss suffered by the Church and proposed the marvelous example of virtue left by Cardinal Barbarigo as an ideal for the entire College of Cardinals.

No one felt the loss more keenly than Lucy, for she had lost a tender father, a generous benefactor, an enlightened guide, the main support of her schools and her Institute. That lonely feeling of her childhood, of being left an orphan in the world, assailed her soul for a brief time again until she remembered that she had a new protector and intercessor in heaven. She had always considered the Cardinal a saint. At his funeral she noticed that this was the universal opinion. His mortal remains were venerated like those of a real Saint. Despite all precautions, people cut off some of his hair and parts of his vestments to keep as relics. The name of Cardinal Barbarigo has remained blessed in all subsequent generations. The fame of his sanctity was formally expressed in 1930 when the diocesan process for his beatification was happily concluded in the city of Montefiascone.

The Cardinal had always intended that Lucy Filippini's Religious Teachers and schools should be a permanent institution of his diocese. Nothing however had been done to guarantee the continued existence of the Institution beyond the testamentary provisions made by the Cardinal, which we shall see proved to be utterly inadequate. Lucy, therefore, had good reason to fear for the existence of her eleven schools scattered throughout the diocese. When the Cardinal's last will was probated and made public, Lucy had a moment of rejoicing on hearing that he had named her schools sole heir to his entire fortune. He instructed executors of his will that immediately upon his demise the entire substance that made up his estate was to be sold and converted into money and securities in the name and for the benefit of the schools. From the interests of the entire sum thus obtained, the schools were to be permanently maintained in the diocese of Montefiascone. He also begged the Bishops his successors to protect this institution and to keep it always in the present flourishing conditions.

Unfortunately for Lucy and her schools the Cardinal had practically died "without his breeches," in the manner he once said every Bishop should die. Because of his many social and charitable works, especially the Diocesan Seminary, the schools and the Religious Teachers and, later, the *Congregation of the Divine Love,* the Cardinal's expenses were often much more than his revenues and he was often forced to borrow to meet his obligations. When his estate was liquidated, it amounted to only 600 gold-dollars. From this sum a yearly interest of some thirty dollars was all that could be expected and with this Lucy was supposed to maintain eleven schools. The amount was utterly inadequate for even one of the eleven schools in those days, when the average amount needed for the yearly support of eleven schools was about fifteen hundred dollars.

In this desperate situation, Lucy as usual took refuge in prayer, her universal remedy in all contingencies.

"When a work is from God"—she used to say in those days—"God Himself feels obliged to protect it."

While resorting to the supernatural means of searching, asking, and knocking with prayer at the door of heavenly mercy, Lucy did not neglect natural means suggested by prudence and experience. Through Father Dominic Longobardi of the Society of the *Pii Operai,* a man highly esteemed by Pope Clement XI, she appealed to the Pontiff himself. The priest reported to the Pope the precarious and desperate conditions of the schools of Montefiascone after the death of Cardinal Barbarigo, adding that many and very great blessings would be lost to the diocese if the schools were closed. The Pope had been previously informed by Cardinal Barbarigo about Lucy's excellent work and apostolate. "By all means," said the Holy Father, "the apostolate of the schools must be continued with undiminished zeal. The necessary means will be provided by the new Bishop."

The Pope appointed Monsignor Sebastian Pompilio Bonaventura Bishop of Montefiascone, to succeed the late Cardinal Barbarigo. Special recommendations were made to the new Bishop by the Pontiff in favor of Lucy's schools and Teachers.

It has always been difficult to succeed a Saint and a genius in any capacity. Bishop Bonaventura was well aware of that difficulty when he was called to the episcopal chair left vacant by Cardinal Barbarigo. His program was simple: to continue in the footsteps of his predecessor; to protect and to consolidate the excellent works of charity and the system of education inaugurated by him, especially the diocesan schools headed by Lucy Filippini. He confirmed Lucy as superintendent of schools and as major superior of the Religious Teachers. Having been informed that the schools were without tangible means of support except for the negligible amount of thirty dollars a year, Bishop Bonaventura began to contribute generously out of his own income towards their operation.

"In the meantime, he placed all the schools under the exalted protection of the Blessed Virgin Mary, instructing the Teachers to have her as their particular advocate in their laudable work of instructing young girls in the holy fear of God. Choosing among the mysteries of the Holy Mother of God one that was allied to the nature of their Institute and that would appeal to the devotion of the Teachers, he designated as their own feast day the Presentation of the Virgin Mary at the Temple of Jerusalem—the day on which the exalted Queen of Heaven had dedicated herself in a particular way to the worship of God and to the service of His House. He wanted them to continue in their devotion to the glorious St. Ignatius Loyola, the Saint who has given to the Church of God a Society whose sons, among other prerogatives, excel especially in the education of youth and in leading young people on the right way to Heaven."[1]

The new Bishop provided not only for the material support of the schools but also for the perpetuation of the spirit, which enshrined in the rules given by the now stilled voice of Barbarigo, must be given a permanent form in writing. He therefore ordered that the rules be put down in writing for eventual publication in printed form so that their observance could be enforced with less difficulty and they could be handed down without changes and confusion to future generations. As mentioned previously, Father Mazzinelli, a priest of the local Seminary, carried out this part of the Bishop's program.

[1] F. DI SIMONE. *Lucia Filippini.* Pag. 60 f.

Lucy saw her prayers answered, her filial trust in Divine Providence rewarded. New and greater trials were on the way —it is true—this was only a temporary relief. Most of her life had been a series of such trials followed by sudden relief and consolation. It would continue with alternate joys and pains to the end of her days but with a crescendo equal to her increased virtue and grace.

Lucy repaid Bishop Bonaventura's generosity and solicitude with the same zeal of obedience and cooperation which she had shown in the past towards the unforgettable Cardinal. She depended upon him in all things, knowing full well that the new Shepherd of the flock was also the new guide sent from Heaven to her soul and to her Institute.

Up to this time, Lucy and her Teachers had followed very conscientiously the method and the order of teaching prescribed by Cardinal Barbarigo. He had insisted repeatedly on the importance of a method whose worth had been proved by many years experience and this method had become almost second nature to the Religious Teachers. Bishop Bonaventura decided to change this traditional system, leaving only a few of the prescriptions of the Cardinal, abolishing the simple questions and answers and adding many long prayers. This new method was inserted into the rules of the Religious Teachers which were first published in 1717.

The change of method caused much disappointment to Lucy, but she suffered silently, making a few respectful observations to the Bishop about the new method. She obeyed however and introduced whatever changes the new method prescribed for the Religious Teachers. Perfect obedience to the new Shepherd would demand much greater sacrifices of her one day and would bring heartaches that would last to the very end of her days.

CHAPTER ELEVEN

LUCY GOES TO ROME.

THE Holy Father, Pope Clement XI, asked Lucy to introduce her school system in Rome. This was the finest recognition and the highest honor bestowed on Lucy Filippini and her Religious Teachers.

Ever since his elevation to St. Peter's Chair Pope Clement XI had admired Cardinal Barbarigo both for the personal holiness of his life and for his apostolic zeal in promoting so many and such excellent works for the education of youth and the sanctification of his flock.

Anxious to extend spiritual reform to the whole Church, the Pope wrote a personal letter to Cardinal Barbarigo asking him for practical advice on a new and universal awakening of the Christian spirit in the Church. The Cardinal submitted a vast and practical program of reform, the Christian education of youth being one of the basic suggestions made in his reply to the Pontiff. As proof thereof he pointed at his own experience with Lucy Filippini's schools for girls. The Cardinal never failed to commend the Religious Teachers for the fine work they were doing in his diocese every time he went to Rome and was received by the Pope. More than once the Pope expressed his desire to have Lucy Filippini open similar schools in Rome for girls of the Eternal City. The Cardinal, however, humbly begged off each time, saying that Lucy could not be replaced at present, because her schools needed a longer period to consolidate and to be firmly and permamently established.

Soon after the death of Cardinal Barbarigo the Pope repeated his request to the Cardinal's successor in Montefiascone, Bishop Bonaventura, through the Pontifical Almoner Alexander Bonaventura, the Bishop's own brother.

The Religious Teachers Filippini were merely a diocesan Institute at the time, the Bishop being their real Superior. Bishop Bonaventura told Lucy of the Holy Father's desire and asked her to go to Rome and to carry out the wishes of His Holiness by opening a school for girls there. Lucy had no worry about the necessary expenses this time, because the Pope's Almoner would take care of everything.

The month of May of the year 1707 found Lucy Filippini in Rome for her first foundation there. Aided by the Fathers of the Society *Pii Operai,* her advisers from the beginning of the Institute, Lucy decided to open her first school in Rome in the Parish of St. Lorenzolo—Little St. Lawrence—near the Convent of the Holy Spirit, on the street of the Golden Keys—*Via delle Chiavi d'oro.* There Lucy had truly entered the road of the Golden Keys by being taken under the exalted protection of the Holy See. It was thus that her Institute came into a unique relation with the Pope's Almoner, their future Superior, and the Institute from diocesan eventually became Pontifical in the sense explained in our first chapter.

Tarquinia, the town that gave old Rome two of its Kings, finally sent to Christian Rome one of its Saints—a burning and shining light—in the person of Lucy Filippini, a girl from Tarquinia. The luster of her example and the radiance of her work grew in splendor with every passing generation, until they reached the glory of Canonization that day in June of 1930. The marble statue of heroic proportions erected to Lucy Filippini in a recess in the middle nave of St. Peter's Basilica in Rome has placed her in the Hall of Fame of the great Saints of the Catholic Church, among the Founders of Religious Orders.

Humble, as usual, were the beginnings of Lucy's first foundation in Rome. The natural sweetness and the charm of her virtue attracted a large number of girls to her school. The profit these girls derived from Lucy's teaching and example is better recounted in the words of a contemporary witness, reported by Lucy's first biographer.

"Lucy impressed not only the school children but also the young ladies who frequented her school with her spirit of real mortification. When she began to teach school in Rome, crowds of young girls were seen flocking to her from all sides. They were attracted by her fervor and the gentleness of her manners. These young women seemed to have no other desire than to mortify themselves. Kneeling at her feet they would ask her for some mortification or punishment for the love of Jesus. Some in fact begged her to have the discipline used on them; some others to be trampled underfoot, thanking the one who did it and kissing her feet; some cheerfully offered their faces to be slapped; others publicly asked pardon of their faults and would trace long crosses on the ground with their tongues. They practiced many other forms of mortification with a fervor that made everybody wonder at Lucy's ability to instill such beautiful spiritual practices in the hearts of her young pupils."[1]

Lucy loved her pupils with that supernatural love described by St. Paul as patient, kind, selfless, long-suffering, full of faith,

[1] F. DI SIMONE. *Lucia Filippini.* Pag. 64 f.

St. Lucy Filippini at the feet of Pope Clement XI.

full of hope, all-enduring, without ambition or secondary motives. Such love together with her cheerful disposition and noble and gentle manners soon captivated the hearts of her pupils
in the City of Rome leaving in them an indelible memory of
her goodness.

In order to introduce these young girls to a practical form
of Christian charity, every Saturday—which was even then a
school holiday—Lucy took some of the most fervent of them
to one of Rome's big Hospitals to show them by example how
to take care of poor sick women, who in those days depended
almost entirely on charity for any service, the nursing system
of our time being completely unknown in those days. While
serving the old women in all their corporal necessities, the girls
did not fail to comfort and to instruct them in the mysteries
of Faith.

With such a shining example of virtue it did not take long
before the Romans realized Lucy's real worth and began to
call her *La Maestra Santa*—The Saintly Teacher—a name later
applied to all her spiritual daughters and even to teachers of
similar Institutes, all because of Lucy's saintly example.

A Religious Teacher of the city of Montefiascone, who had
been one of Lucy's first pupils in Rome, did not feel any special
attraction for Lucy at first, because of her peculiar religious
habit so different from those commonly seen in the Eternal City.
As soon as she began to frequent Lucy's school and to listen
to her conducting the various devotional exercises, her attitude
changed.

"I became so attached to her"—she said—"that I cried in
order to obtain my parents' permission to stay with her. She
seemed so much like a saint to me. The special method she
followed at school and the prayer she said with us pleased me

so much that I was almost beside myself. For this reason I never missed school and sometimes I had the great satisfaction of remaining there overnight."

Lucy had always been an apostle, in addition to being a teacher. Grown women of that section of the city began to frequent her school on the Street of the Golden Keys to take part in meditation and other pious exercises morning and evening. Some of these ladies must have informed Lucy about a disorderly house in that district, near Trajan's Forum, not far from her school. Lucy was deeply grieved and distressed on hearing this, not only because the unfortunate inmates of that house were themselves in danger of eternal damnation but also on account of the scandal given by them to some of her pupils who had to pass their place daily in coming to school. She tried every means known to her in order to save those women and actually succeeded in converting two of them. In order to take these two away from the occasion of sin and to confirm them in their resolve of amendment, Lucy took them to her own house and kept them secluded in a room under the school.

Had Lucy known the tense situation existing in Rome in those days following the suppression of Quietism after the punishment of Michael Molinos, she might have acted otherwise perhaps in her missionary activity outside the school both here in Rome and elsewhere. A fierce and dangerous storm was started by malicious or ignorant people who, at such times, see danger everywhere. They began to spread rumors about Lucy, saying that she was both a follower and a teacher of Quietistic doctrines. A few Ecclesiastics picked up these rumors and, unable or unwilling to judge or discern between true and false rumors, denounced Lucy to the Holy Office for teaching the doctrines of Michael Molinos. Lucy's friends trembled for her safety, seeing her already locked up in the dreaded prisons of the Holy Office of those days, with very serious consequences for her schools and her Institute. She was informed about her accusers and the charges of false doctrines and immoral practices brought against her and she was warned to be on her guard against the Ecclesiastics.

Beginning with Our Blessed Lord Himself, it has been the fate of many of His Saints to be thus misunderstood and falsely accused before Ecclesiastical tribunals. Even when declared innocent of all charges—as was the case with our Lucy—a dark cloud of suspicion follows them through life. It was so with our Lucy. Denunciations and charges were repeated several times against her later in life. The Holy Office kept an eye on Lucy as long as she lived. There is hardly any more bitter trial for a Servant of God than to be suspected by a representative of the very Church they serve with utmost devotion and purity of faith.

Lucy was asked to appear before the Vicar of the Holy Office in the city of Todi to give an account of her doctrine and her spiritual practices, especially the form of her mental prayer. In the month of May of the year 1719, she had given a spiritual retreat for women in the town of Scansano. Some zealots denounced her and she had to appear before the Vicar of the Holy Office of that town who had been officially requested to examine the charges and make a report to Rome. It is very instructive to read the account—rather involved in its original Italian—given by the Vicar, because it contains important details about Lucy's apostolate. Here is our translation:

"On the evening of May 14 of this year, two strange women arrived here in Scansano and stayed, for eight days at the house belonging to Lieutenant Pippi by themselves with no one else living in the same place. . . . They had been accompanied to

Scansano by the Curate of Monte Marano who remained here for the eight days that the two women were in town, the Curate staying at the Pastor's house. . . .

"One of the women was called *Signora Lucia* and the other, Santa. Lucia was about thirty-five years of age [she was actually forty-seven] of ordinary appearance and she is the Superior of the Conservatory for young ladies in the city of Montefiascone. The other, called Santa, is about twenty-six or twenty-seven years old and rather handsome. She is the Superior of the Conservatory of Pitigliano where she resides. During those eight days they gave spiritual exercises twice a day—morning and evening—four hours each time. These exercises were given in the building used as Seminary.

"Said exercises consisted of one and a half hour of spiritual reading from a book by P. Pinamonti. This was followed by a point of meditation or mental prayer, from the Meditations by Ruggieri. The points of meditation were on the Last Things: Death, on the first day; Judgment, on the second; Hell, on the third; Paradise, on the fourth. Having read the point of meditation, she ordered the window closed and after a brief pause for reflection she pointed out the fruit in the manner of an exhortation. Some of those women were often moved to tears by her words. All the women of the town took part in the exercises. Most of the local priests and laymen in great number came to the exercises, listening in from an adjoining room which communicated by a door with the room occupied by the women. I myself was present at all the exercises. Both the spiritual reading and the meditation were made by the Signora Lucia. As soon as the meditation was concluded, the other named Santa sang a spiritual hymn with a beautiful voice like that of a trained singer. Regarding their permission to give this retreat, I was assured by the Curate of Monte Marano that they had obtained it from the Bishop. The same retreat had been given by them in Monte Marano before they came here. . . .

"No disorder of any kind occurred during these exercises, except that some of the women fainted because of the heat or the crowded room.

"In faith, etc. I, Nicholas Ranieri, Vicar for the Holy Office in the Territory of Scansano."

On receipt of this report, the Holy Office requested further information about Lucy from the Bishop of Montefiascone. In his reply the Bishop repeated the facts known to everybody in reference to Lucy Filippini's virtue, superior intelligence and courage. He also called the attention of the Holy Office to Lucy's schools in the City of Rome, opened by request of His Holiness and supported by him.

It may appear strange today that a department of the Holy See should harbor suspicions about Lucy's activity and harass her with repeated questioning when the Holy Father himself had such high opinion of her. The attitude of the Holy Office will be better understood if we remember the scandal and the confusion created by the erroneous doctrines and the immoral practices of the Quietists which were still rampant in many parts of Europe, Spain, France, and Italy, and especially in Rome. Most of the seventeenth century and part of the eighteenth was the period of history that saw the spread of Quietism in one form or another affecting not only many of the faithful but also a number of priests, many religious communities, some Bishops and even some Cardinals. The one who caused the greatest and widest scandal was the Spanish priest Michael Molinos, born December 21, 1640. As a priest he came to Rome preceded by a great reputation as an experienced and assiduous

Confessor. He was esteemed by many distinguished dignitaries of the Eternal City for a number of years. Among his friends were several members of the Sacred College of Cardinals, like Colloredo, Ciceri, Petrucci, Casanata, Carpegna, Azzolini, and even the very pious Odeschalchi who later became Pope Inno-

Lucy Gives a Retreat to the Women of Scansano

cent XI. In the beginning, Molinos enjoyed the confidence of the Pope himself.

It is hard to say whether this was a case of schizophrenia or of vulgar duplicity, but the fact remains that Michael Molinos did lead a double life, saintly and spiritual in public, sensual and immoral in private. According to his absurd doctrine of absolute passivity and quiet, however, there was neither immorality in his actions nor inconsistency between his doctrine and his conduct.

The basic principle of the Quietistic doctrine would make Christian perfection consist in absolute passivity and in the suppression of all spiritual activity and all moral endeavor. After making such an act of passivity the Quietist left everything to God for the rest of his life, not indeed in the common sense of self-abandonment in the hands of God, but as an excuse for declaring himself free of any obligation of all responsibility for his actions, even when these were manifestly sinful. According to the Quietists "every action is an imperfection," not only in prayer but in everything. Their so-called prayer of quiet or acquired contemplation is a farce when compared to the same form of mental prayer as taught by St. Teresa and other spiritual writers. Entire Religious communities began to adopt this sort of nirvanic passivity in prayer, abandoning all the traditional devotions and exercises, growing remiss and apathetic towards all their duties and obligations. Nearly a hundred books dealing with spiritual matter published during this period were infected with Quietism and were placed on the Index of Forbidden Books. The most famous of these works is Michael Molinos' book *The Spiritual Guide* "which disengaging the soul guides it by the interior way to the acquisition of perfect contemplation and to the rich treasure of interior peace." Sixty-eight propositions taken from this book were condemned as erroneous, false, scandalous, etc., and the book was placed on the Index. There was too an esoteric doctrine practiced by Molinos which he did not dare put in his book. In virtue of this doctrine, he committed many immoral actions, adulteries, sacrileges, etc. Between the years 1675 and 1687, he never went to Sacramental Confession. When the truth finally came out, especially through the efforts of Father Paolo Segneri, S.J., Molinos was brought to trial before the Holy Office. He confessed to his crimes and was condemned to life imprisonment—in a Dominican Monastery in Rome—where he died penitent, December 28, 1697.

The memory of these facts and the effect of the great scandal were still very much alive when Lucy arrived in Rome. Among Molinos' belongings was found a vast correspondence with people in almost every part of the world. Thousands of letters, from persons in every walk of life, gave evidence to his pernicious influence and to the magnitude of the evil. Cardinal Petrucci who, in good faith perhaps, had written a book in defense of Molinos had to appear before the Sacred Inquisition but was released. In spite of all these measures, Quietism was still rampant during the first three decades of the eighteenth century. In the year 1710 Father Joseph Beccarelli of Milan was condemned to forced labor for life because of his Quietistic errors. A certain Sister Teresa was punished and her Molinistic writings burnt in Sicily in 1724. In France Quietism continued for a longer period where it assumed a new form—the Semi-Quietism of Father LaCombe, Madame Guyon, etc. In view of these facts the Holy Office had to act every time a denunciation was made against any person, no matter how respectable and holy.

In Lucy's case there were some exterior circumstances which, may have appeared, if not incriminating, at least such as to offer ground for suspicion. Her spirituality had been influenced by the Society of the *Pii Operai,* who had acted as Confessors and advisers since the beginning of her Institute. The Superior General of the *Pii Operai,* Father Anthony Torres, having been denounced to the Holy Office as a follower of Molinos, had been forbidden to preach or to hear confession, and lived in seclusion. The next Superior in Rome, Father L. Sabbatini, was publicly called a Quietist—with how much foundation is not said.

In addition, every gathering of faithful for the purpose of practicing mental prayer, was looked upon with great suspicion, because of the many similar gatherings of Quietists for the exercise of their so-called prayer of passive contemplation. Lucy's activity in giving the points of mental prayer to women could have been easily misunderstood as a Quietistic gathering. The keeping of the two women of bad reputation—even though reformed—in her house added even greater weight to the suspicions.

Probably Lucy had never heard anything about Quietism in her life before coming to Rome. In her innocence and simplicity and in full possession of truth and sound doctrine, she did not worry about charges and denunciations made against her. She was unafraid and never stopped her missionary work for fear of being misunderstood and punished. She thus experienced another of the Beatitudes, that of being falsely accused and persecuted for the sake of justice.

Luckily her residence in Rome was cut short by developments in the schools of Montefiascone. Most of the Teachers she had left behind were now sick and discouraged. Lucy's presence was needed to remedy a critical situation. Before leaving Rome she gave the habit of the Religious Teachers to a talented young lady, Miss Margaret Setoli, who was to carry on, taking Lucy's place as Teacher.

The importance of this first foundation, however, was such that Lucy did not think it proper to leave its direction in the hands of a young person. To give more prestige to the school, she invited her old friend Rose Venerini to come to Rome from Viterbo and take the direction of the school. -Encouraged by her spiritual director Father Martinelli, S.J., Rose Venerini accepted Lucy's invitation and went to Rome, arriving there at the beginning of December of that year 1707.

Very happy at Rose's coming, Lucy prepared for her return to Montefiascone. When the pupils understood that she was leaving them, there was such sadness and crying that Lucy stole away very early one day in order not to increase their pain at her departure.

Finding that she had left that morning, the girls began to cry so bitterly that poor Rose Venerini did not know how to comfort them.

"What are you crying for?"—she asked—"Is it perhaps on account of the Signora Lucia?"

"Why shouldn't we cry, now that we have lost her?"—they replied.

CHAPTER TWELVE

LUCY'S ROMAN SCHOOLS.

THE difference in the methods and the personalities of the two saintly teachers, Lucy Filippini and Rose Venerini, never appeared more clearly than in the direction of the first school that was opened in Rome in 1707. Immediately after Lucy's departure from the Eternal City, when the school she had founded was placed under the direction of Rose Venerini, the number of pupils began to decline so alarmingly that before long the school was practically deserted.

It is not easy to say whether this sudden lack of interest toward the school by the pupils was the result of Rose's method and personality or of the girls' great affection for Lucy. It is a fact, however, that Rose Venerini who had never fully agreed with the school method of Cardinal Barbarigo was even more opposed to the changes and additions made by Bishop Bonaventura. Discarding Lucy's method, which the girls had followed with great profit and satisfaction, Rose Venerini adopted her own followed in all her schools. The girls did not find the new system and the new teacher much to their liking and they began to stay away from school.

When the Pope's Almoner, Alexander Bonaventura, returned for a visit of the school, he was greatly surprised to find it almost empty. He lost no time in looking into the distressing

situation. He wrote immediately to his brother, Bishop Bonaventura, asking him to send two of Lucy's Religious Teachers
from Montefiascone to take care of the school because Rose
Venerini had expressed her intention of returning to Viterbo.
The Bishop complied with the request and sent two of Lucy's
Teachers to Rome. With their arrival the school began to
flourish again.

Rose Venerini had remained in Rome only four months, but
even though disappointed at her failure, she saw the great opportunity to open schools of her own in the Capital of Christen-
dom, run according to her own system. While preparing for
her first foundation in Rome, Rose Venerini was the guest for
several years of Lucy's spiritual daughters who did everything
to please her and to be of assistance to her. In spite of this, she
did not seem to feel at home with them. Letters written to her
spiritual director during those years expressed great uneasiness,
saying that she felt as if she were living in a desert there, having
no one in whom she could confide.

By this time Bishop Bonaventura had come to the conclusion
that there could be no further cooperation between the two
school systems. He had been displeased to have Rose Venerini
discard the system he had approved for Lucy, and knowing well
that Rose would never adopt any other system but her own, he
decided that in the future her assistance would not be asked
again by Lucy or her daughters.

Whatever moral union there had been between the two
branches of the *Maestre Pie* now came to an end. There was a
complete separation between the work of Lucy Filippini and that
of Rose Venerini, a separation meant for the good of their respective Institutes. It did not come from either woman but from
Lucy's Superior. This separation was later acknowledged and

confirmed by the Holy See. Lucy had always been fond of Rose Venerini and could not help feeling the pain by this official severance of whatever ties had existed between them. This was another sacrifice imposed by obedience and she made it with her customary humble submission, accepting it as a cross. In a letter she wrote at this time to Father Martinelli, S.J., she said: "I hope some good will come out of this, since our dear Lord has so ordained it through our Superiors."[1]

The first school at the street of the Golden Keys was transferred to a house near the Church of St. Agata dei Goti, in the parish of the Madonna dei Monti. This became the center and a sort of motherhouse of all the other Roman schools founded by Lucy, and it remained so for a long time.

There were eight schools opened by Lucy in the city of Rome by the time of her death in 1732. Besides the one already mentioned, there was a school at the Quattro Fontane, one in Trastevere, one in the Via Frattina, one at St. Peter's, one at St. Lawrence in Lucina, one on the Piazza Pollarola, and one near St. Andrea della Valle.

At this time both Lucy Filippini's schools and the two that Rose Venerini had opened in Rome were under the jurisdiction of the Pope's Almoner. In time, the Venerini Teachers passed to the jurisdiction of the Apostolic Datary but the Filippini Teachers remained under the Almoner as before.

The monthly salary paid each teacher by the Almoner in those days was thirty-five Paoli or about seven gold dollars. There were more than a thousand pupils in the eight schools opened by Lucy in Rome. Many other schools were opened by her spiritual daughters in the course of time, both in Rome itself and in its suburbs.

[1] P. BERGAMASCHI. *Le Origini.* Pag. 91.

It was Lucy's wish that all the Religious Teachers working in the other seven schools of Rome should regard the first school, the one of the Madonna dei Monti, as their spiritual center. Each week-end was to be spent there by all the Teachers in a happy and holy reunion for an exchange of experiences and to find encouragement and edification under a well regulated discipline. On these week-ends they visited the sacred Shrines of Rome and assisted at the sacred functions of the great Roman Basilicas, thus refreshing their spirit and reviving their fervor for another week of work in the classroom. On Monday morning, each teacher returned to her post resuming her work with new zest and courage. There is a deep psychological reason behind this practice started by St. Lucy Filippini. Small communities soon forget regular discipline and lose contact both with the spirit and the body of the Institute. One soon becomes a victim of discouragement in a community of two or three members. Numbers in themselves often are an inspiration, and the good example of many is a dynamic force not easy to resist.

It was in this central house and school in the parish of the Madonna dei Monti, towards the end of the eighteenth century, that another future Saint and a great mystic soul received her schooling and her first religious instruction and training by Lucy's Religious Teachers. The girl's name was Anna Maria Taigi. Imbued with the religious spirit of prayer, mortification, and practical charity taught by Lucy to the first pupils of that school, Anna Maria became the "valiant woman," a model Christian wife and mother that the Church has proposed to the veneration of the faithful in our own days. In this school she learned to read and to meditate on the mysteries of our Faith. They became the food and comfort of her spirit amidst the many trials of her life. She had distinguished herself at school in the learning of Catechism, and as for prayers, we have the testimony of her own daughter Sophie who said at the first process for her mother's Beatification,

"She could recite the Psalms by heart; she knew as much as a Curate, and she could have been a teacher to all."

Anna Maria Taigi retained a grateful and pleasant remembrance of the years spent at that school because when the time came she would send her own doughters to no other school than those of the *Maestre Pie Filippini.*

In addition to the eight schools founded by Lucy, two other places were placed in charge of her Religious Teachers in Rome during her lifetime; the Conservatory of the so-called *Zoccolette* and another school in the Via Graziosa. The number of new schools opened by the Religious Teachers in Rome has increased with the years in proportion to the increased population of the City.

Among the new schools opened there, mention should be made of the one at the *Tre Fontane*—the Three Fountains—by request of Pope Benedict XV. Some distance outside the southern side of the ancient city walls and a little over a mile beyond St. Paul's Basilica on the Ostian Way is the place sanctified by the blood of the Apostle St. Paul where he was beheaded. The Romans called this place *Ad Aquas Salvias,* implying the presence of health-giving waters in that section.

According to a very ancient tradition, a fountain of waters sprung up at each of the three spots where the head of the Apostle touched the ground after being severed by the sword of the executioner. A church was later built there enclosing the three fountains, hence its present name. An ancient Abbey of Trappists, once honored by the presence of the great St. Bernard of

Clairvaux, is nearby and another church containing innumerable relics of Holy Martyrs is on the same hallowed ground.

The Religious Teachers Filippini were asked to open a school in this sparsely populated section. They did so with their customary system and devotion. The once malaria-infested district of the Roman Campagna was planted with eucalyptus trees by the silent monks of the Abbey over a generation ago. The trees have grown into a stately forest, in whose foliage the evening wind seems to sing an endless hymn of praise and thanksgiving to Christ the glorious King of the Apostles and the Martyrs.

There is a hill in this eucalyptus grove and on the hillside a grotto. When the devastating Second World War reached Rome, soldiers were seen by the Trappists using this grotto for shameful purposes, and thieves also came here to divide their stolen goods. Then something happened.

On April 12, 1947, a streetcar conductor, named Bruno Cornacchiola, a fallen-away Catholic—then a Protestant Minister—had promised his three children, a ten-year-old girl, Isola, two boys, Charles seven, and Gianfranco four, a trip to Ostia Mare, the Roman beach, that afternoon. They missed the train at St. Paul's station, and not wanting to disappoint the children, Bruno took them to the eucalyptus grove at the Tre Fontane to play ball. An open space near the famous grotto was a good play ground. Suddenly the ball was lost and could not be found. Bruno who was sitting by himself working at another of his vitriolic attacks against the Catholic Church and the Immaculate Conception—his favorite targets—put paper and pencil in his pocket to join the children in the search. He took Charles with himself and left little Gianfranco with his daughter, Isola.

Bruno kept calling to the little boy every few minutes to be sure that the child had not wandered away on uneven ground, full of holes and ditches. The boy answered regularly for awhile, but when no answer came to several later repeated calls, Bruno became alarmed and went back to investigate. To his surprise he found little Gianfranco on his knees—a thing he had never taught his children to do—in front of the grotto, his hands joined in prayer, a happy smile on his face. He seemed to be talking to someone within the grotto, repeating over and over again *"Bella Signora! ... Bella Signora! ..."*—Lovely Lady! ... Lovely Lady! ... The child was not even baptized at the time, and he had not been taught such expressions in the house where Our Blessed Lady was only insulted and blasphemed. In the meantime, Isola had been picking flowers nearby, paying no attention to what her little brother was saying. Bruno called her to the grotto. When she came, Bruno asked her and the boy Charles, who was standing at his side, whether they saw anything in that grotto, because the little Gianfranco would not stop talking to the "Lovely Lady" and would not answer any questions even when they shook him. Both Isola and Charles said they saw nothing. The word was hardly spoken when Isola fell to her knees, joined her hands, and with her eyes fixed on a point in the grotto, began to exclaim "Lovely Lady!"

Bruno, for a moment, thought that he had found the solution. It was just a prank! The children must have agreed to play this trick on him. Satisfied with this idea, he turned to Charles still standing at his side and half smiling said, "What about you? When are you going to kneel down?"

"Oh, go on!" answered the boy in scorn at such a suggestion. He had hardly spoken when he too bent his knees, joined his hands and repeated the same words as his brother and sister. At this the father was filled with great fear. The children had become stiff, very pale, with eyes dilated. Unable to see anything in the shadowy grotto himself, he could not explain the phenomenon except as a diabolical trick. Fearing for the safety of his children he cried out: "Lord, save us!" That prayer had been scarcely uttered when he felt two powerful hands on his shoulders, forcing him down on his knees.

A veil seemed to fall from Bruno's eyes; the dark grotto disappeared; he felt very light, as if freed of the burden of his body, and he was flooded with a light not of this world. In this light a figure appeared, the figure of a lady of transcendent beauty, an oriental with an olive complexion but of a majestic and dignified loveliness. Her black hair not parted in front showed a little under the cloak which fell from her head down both sides to her feet with the front open. The color of her cloak was a tender green. Her snow-white dress was held by a rose-colored sash which reached from her waist down to her knees. Her bare feet rested on a rock of tufa. The "Beautiful Lady" with an expression both sweet and sad on her face, held a small book with a grey cover in her right hand and with her left she pointed at a black robe near a broken cross on the ground.

The three children saw her lips moving but heard no sound. Bruno, their father, heard a voice, the like of which—he said— was never heard in this world.[2]

---

[2] These and several other details were learned by the writer from Bruno Cornacchiola himself in the month of July, 1949. The Church has not yet given official approval to this apparition. Numerous extraordinary cures have been reported at the grotto, and also through the use of earth taken from there.

"I am the one who is in the Trinity Divine. I am the Virgin of the Revelation. You are persecuting me. It is enough now! Enter the sacred fold, the court of Heaven on earth. The nine Fridays which you observed before you entered the way of deceit have saved you."

These words of the Lady to Bruno were only the introduction to a very long message which lasted from 4:10 to 5:30 that April afternoon, a message Bruno felt constantly running in his mind like a phonograph record until he had put it down in writing up to its last word: *"Amore*—love," then it stopped. This message was then given to the competent Ecclesiastical authority in Rome for study.

The Lady gave Bruno a sign to prove that this was "a divine reality and not a Satanic illusion." For over two weeks he waited for the fulfillment of the sign, and when he was becoming despondent, the sign was fulfilled in all its particulars. "The voice of Heaven"—said Bruno—"had told me: 'In order to assure you that this vision is a divine reality and not a Satanic illusion, as many would have you believe, I give you this sign: Go through the churches and through the streets of the city. You are to address the first priest whom you meet in a church or on the street with these words: Father, I must talk to you! To the one who replies: Ave Maria, my son, what do you wish? —you are to say whatever comes to your mind. The priest will direct you to someone who will receive your abjuration with these words: He will do for your case! ... On April 28 having entered the Church of All Saints on the new Appian Way, I finally met a priest—Don Mario Frosi—who answered my question with the words: Ave Maria, my son! and directed me to his confrere—Don Gilberto Carniel—who had recently received a convert from Protestantism into the Church."

During those two weeks between April 12 and 28, Bruno had asked dozens of priests on the street, in churches and even on street cars. When he did not receive the answer indicated by the Virgin, he simply excused himself. "I began to look like a fool and was becoming discouraged." The Virgin of the Revelation had advised him to be prudent and not to become discouraged if people refused to believe him, adding,

"Even with the earth of this sinful place—alluding to the former usage of the grotto—"I will work great miracles for the conversion of unbelievers." She asked that prayers be offered for "the unity of all Christians."

What happened to the lost ball? When the vision was over and the four were standing there in front of the grotto, Bruno saw the ball resting near his right foot. They left it there, and never played there again.

Bruno and his whole family returned to the Catholic Church, "the Sacred Fold, the Court of Heaven on earth." Bruno was so changed by this vision that he became a new man in every sense of the word. Asked the date of his birth in one of the many official questionings, he was inspired to answer: "I was born on April 12, 1947."

Many times after the first apparition, Bruno visited the grotto, now hallowed, of the Tre Fontane. During the following month of May the Lady appeared to him three times amidst heavenly splendors, leaving always a fragrance of lilies. On the third of these apparitions, May 30, 1947, she spoke again:

"Tell my beloved daughters, the Religious Teachers Filippini, to pray for all the unbelievers, especially for those of this district."[2] Isola, the girl who saw the beautiful Lady, was entrusted to the care of Lucy Filippini's daughters.

There is a school of the Religious Teachers Filippini near the ancient monastery of the Tre Fontane. It was a sign of predilection for them to be singled out among other Religious communities by the Lovely Lady with a message for their prayers.

The schools that Lucy first opened in Rome continued her apostolic work in the Eternal City, attracting the blessings of Heaven and also the gratitude of men to our own time.

CHAPTER THIRTEEN

TRIUMPHS AND TRIALS.

"I wish I could be in every corner of the earth and cry out to all the people, no matter what their age, sex, and position in life, and tell them: 'Love our God! Love our God!'—O dear Lord, why not grant me to become many Lucies to carry your glory to all the world!" These noble sentiments of Lucy Filippini, worthy of an apostle of Christ, found their practical expression in her missionary activity and in what we call today Catholic Action. In this respect Lucy Filippini seems to stand alone among the great women of history and the great Saints of her sex. Many saintly women have manifested an apostolic spirit and manly courage, yet none ever went out giving missions from town to town to the end of their life like Lucy. Even though these missions, in the form of a spiritual retreat of eight or ten consecutive days were meant for women only, their effect was felt by the entire population. Occasionally men and even priests went to listen from an adjoining room, and they derived no less profit from them than the women. On one occasion two men, out of curiosity, climbed to the roof of the house in which Lucy was talking to the women. Deeply moved at her words, they went to confession and one of them abandoned the world in order to serve God alone.

As long as Cardinal Barbarigo lived, Lucy was not permitted to extend her activity—opening new schools and giving retreats —outside his territory, regardless of the many requests made to her by other Bishops. After his death, however, she was first permitted—even commanded—to open schools in Rome, and later in other dioceses.

After her return from the Eternal City in December 1707, Lucy gave her immediate attention to the sick members of her Institute. With her presence and her maternal care they soon recovered their health and were able to resume work in the classroom. Lucy then started a general visitation of all the schools of the diocese, a few of which had been closed during her absence and few more were struggling for existence. She reopened those that had been closed and placed the others on a more solid basis. In a short time all the schools were once more flourishing. Returning to her headquarters in Montefiascone, Lucy began to feel the urge of extending her apostolate to other places outside the diocese. She had always worked within the northern section of Latium, now with her Bishop's permission she extended her schools and her missionary activity to other regions and other dioceses.

The Grand Duke of Tuscany, Cosimo III, had visited Lucy's school of Montefiascone in the days of Cardinal Barbarigo. On that occasion the Grand Duke expressed his admiration for the *Maestra Santa* together with the wish to have her open similar schools for the young daughters of his subjects. Availing himself now of the new policy introduced by Bishop Bonaventura, the Grand Duke renewed his request. With her Bishop's approval, Lucy gladly accepted.

One of the first schools opened by Lucy in Tuscany was at Monte Marano to which the Grand Duke assigned special an-

The Grand Duke of Tuscany Visits Lucy's School

nual revenues. He wanted Lucy Filippini to take the direction of all his schools for girls. He also gave Lucy full permission to conduct retreats for women throughout Tuscany. On a visit to the school at Pitigliano, Lucy fell sick. On hearing this the Grand Duke from Florence, sent her three very elaborate boxes of medicines and medical aids as a token of his esteem and gratitude.

The school of Pitigliano in the former Grand Duchy of Tuscany deserves special mention because of Lucy's successful mission there. A popular missionary, St. Leonard of Porto Maurizio —a contemporary of Lucy preached a mission in this town in the year 1712. In spite of the many conversions among the people, St. Leonard had not succeeded in breaking down the excessive vanity of the women in their extreme manner of dress. Soon after Lucy arrived in Pitigliano to open a school, she announced a retreat for women. This was her usual system, a new school opening with a retreat for the mothers and the young ladies. Once the school was well established the ladies were expected to keep in contact with the school especially at the time of meditation and other religious practices.

The women of Pitigliano came to Lucy's retreat adorned with flowers, ribbons, and jewels, as if for a ball. Lucy saw everything but said nothing. She began the retreat with such fervor of spirit that after the first three or four meditations the retreatants, seeing themselves in the light of the truths of Faith, began to feel ashamed and to weep over their vanities and their worldliness. They then changed to more modest dress in conformity with the Christian spirit. From then on, there were no more flowers in the hair, no more ribbons; gloves even, and bracelets were discarded by the ladies after that retreat. A change so radical and so permanent evidenced Lucy's power which had succeeded where the great Leonard of Porto Maurizio had failed.

Similar also were the circumstances and the results of another retreat in the town of Scansano, in the district of Siena. Here too, Lucy had been preceded by St. Leonard. He had preached a mission there bringing about a moral reform. The women of that town had resolved to abandon their frills and to dress more modestly. However, there had been no real conversion for no sooner had St. Leonard left town than the ladies returned to their former vanities. At the conclusion of Lucy's retreat in Scansano, however, the ladies not only put away all their vanities but they never wore them again. A young lady—who later became a Religious Teacher—arrived in Scansano sometime after Lucy had given her retreat there, carrying a bouquet of flowers in her hand. On seeing them, her own sister who lived there became alarmed.

"For the love of Heaven, sister, do not let anybody see you carrying those flowers; you would be a scandal. Ever since Signora Lucia's retreat in this town, we no longer wear ribbons, flowers, or any other vanities as we used to." Another retreat given by Lucy in Scansano, seven years later, has been already reported previously in the words of the Vicar of the Holy Office, Nicholas Ranieri. Lucy's retreats were almost like a popular mission and the fruits were the same, at times even more abundant and more enduring. The women of the town of Veroli were so taken by the power of her words and the charm of her manners that they told everyone that Lucy had stolen their hearts.

"We could go without food and without sleep for the joy of listening to her and staying with her."

At times, however, Lucy had to overcome prejudice and ill feeling against her, before bringing the women to a more Christian form of living. Once when she entered the town of Onano for a retreat, she was received with insults; some even threw stones at her to drive her out of town. Lucy remained calm and undismayed. She began her retreat with great patience and humility. Before the retreat was over the women who had insulted her came to apologize. When she left town, the people all came out with her, some even crying at having insulted a Saint.

The salutary effects of Lucy's missionary activity were not so much the result of natural gifts and a charming personality but of personal holiness and charismatic graces bestowed upon her. Violent storms that threatened death and destruction were stilled suddenly at the voice of her prayer. Extraordinary cures were effected simply with the sign of the cross made by Lucy. Such was the case of a woman whose arm was to be amputated because of a gangrenous infection. The surgical instruments were ready for the painful operation—there was no anesthesia in those days—when Lucy moved by compassion for the poor woman came, made the sign of the cross on the infected arm, curing it at once and completely so that the dreadful operation became unnecessary. In like manner Lucy cured another woman in the town of Marta. In both these cases Lucy humbly attributed the miraculous cures to the intercession of Cardinal Barbarigo who by this time had died.

Returning one day from Rome to Montefiascone in company of another Religious Teacher, both women were saved from drowning by Lucy's prayer. While crossing the dangerous bridge of Sutri, the coachman whipped the horses. The carriage in which they were riding was kicked by the frightened beasts and thrown from the bridge into the river. Seeing the imminent danger, Lucy joined her hands in prayer and cried out with faith: "Jesus and Mary, help us!" The Lord heard her call. The carriage stopped long enough in its fall to let Lucy and her companion step out safely before tumbling into the river.

Charismatic graces are given occasionally to apostolic souls to aid them in the propagation of faith, the conversion of unbelievers, the edification of the faithful. The gifts of prophecy and of knowing the secrets of conscience were found in Lucy to a high degree. To a young postulant of her Institute who thought she had tuberculosis and was therefore afraid of being dismissed, Lucy said:

"Yes, we will give you the habit. Your sickness is simply a temptation of the devil. You will become a Religious Teacher." And so it happened.

Lucy was forewarned by several days that the money deposited in the *Monte di Pietà* of Montefiascone would be stolen. Some of the funds belonging to her schools were deposited there. Because of her foreknowledge, she went to the *Monte di Pietà* one day and asked the priest in charge of the deposits:

"Would the depositors lose their money if thieves were to steal it from the *Monte di Pietà?*"

"They certainly would"—answered the priest—"if the stealing could not be attributed to any negligence on my part."

"If that's the case,"—said Lucy smiling—"I want all my money back!"

A few days later the *Monte di Pietà* was robbed and all the depositors, except Lucy, lost their money.

When visiting her schools, she revealed the most hidden disorders and abuses before anybody could have told her. Her

Lucy Before the Tribunal of the Holy Office

school girls avoided her presence whenever they were conscious of having commited a fault, because they knew that they could not hide it from Lucy.

Another phenomenon revealing the mystical trend and the ardent devotion of Lucy's soul happened in the town of Pitigliano. Lucy's love for her Eucharistic Lord and her burning desire to receive Him in Holy Communion has been praised by all her biographers. Because of her love for the Blessed Sacrament of the Altar she had great reverence and respect for the priests, never thinking of judging nor of condemning them.

"Priests are not men but Angels of Paradise," she used to say. In a century when Jansenism had made Holy Communion a rare practice, Lucy received our Lord every day, except one during the week, desisting on this day only because her spiritual director had advised it.

Out of devotion for St. Francis of Assisi, early one morning she went to Mass at St. Francis' Church on top of a hill near the town of Pitigliano. Lucy and her companion had been kneeling there in the church for quite awhile before the priest came out to say Mass. Instead of going to the altar of the Blessed Sacrament, the priest went to a side altar. Lucy felt disappointed because she wanted to receive Holy Communion during Mass. She, nevertheless, prepared herself with her customary devotion as if to receive our Lord. At the breaking of the sacred Host, the priest noticed that the fragment he had dropped into the chalice completely disappeared. Instead of falling into the chalice, it was deposited on Lucy's tongue. The priest, alarmed at the disappearance of the sacred particle, looked everywhere to find it but without success. After Mass the priest returned to the altar to search again for the missing fragment. Seeing his anguish, Lucy felt bound to reveal to him the mystery of the disappearance. She walked up to the priest and humbly told him that the fragment had not been lost but had been given to her for her Communion that morning. A similar incident is reported in the life of St. Catherine of Siena, a Saint Lucy resembled in many ways. In such ways our Lord comforted Lucy in her missionary work and helped make her efforts towards the salvation of souls more efficacious and her name more honored.

While our Lord thus seconded Lucy's activities, the enemy of mankind used every effort to stop her. The idea of retreats given by a woman at a time when any novelty in spiritual matters was looked upon with suspicion was enough to create doubts and difficulties. While in the diocese of Todi to open the school of Acquasparta, Lucy gave a retreat to the women of the city of Todi. The local Bishop, Cardinal Philip Gualterio, who had received her with great satisfaction, became suspicious when he heard that she was giving a retreat to the women of Todi. In order to reassure himself, Lucy was examined by the local representatives of the Holy Office about her method of mental prayer and the other religious exercises of the retreat. Undisturbed by their questioning and its implications, Lucy answered in all humility and sincerity. The Theologians found nothing to justify any suspicions. Her doctrine and her religious exercises were Catholic, and corresponded to sound Catholic tradition. In the meantime the learned men, too, felt the power of her words and the charm of her candid soul. They had heard of nothing any more efficacious for the conversion of sinners than the spiritual exercises given by Lucy Filippini. She was, therefore, given ample scope to continue her mission for the good of the Church and the salvation of souls. Similar suspicions and denunciations were repeated again and again, but Lucy was always cleared of them, coming out with more merit and new courage to carry on.

Because of such false accusations and denunciations, some of her spiritual daughters had to suffer similar vexations. Evil people publicly insulted them several times. At Arlena a man attempted to kill some of them. Lucy had opened a school in the town of Piansano in the days of Cardinal Barbarigo. She placed this school under the care of two very zealous Religious Teachers, Anna and Livia Lottieri. The priest in this town, was the son of a well-to-do and noble family, very learned but lacking that Christian humility and kindness which are the marks of true wisdom and nobility of soul. This priest conducted a campaign against the two saintly Teachers accusing them of being ignorant and of teaching heretical doctrines. At the hour when the Teachers gave the points of meditation, Don Parri used to send a Capuchin Brother to listen in and to insult them, saying that they were teaching errors. Once on Holy Thursday when one of the Lottieri sisters was about to enter the confessional, a Capuchin Father Confessor who dined daily with Don Parri became so infuriated that he began to accuse her publicly and loudly of ignorance and heresy, adding that he would denounce her and her sister to the Holy Office. This, of course, was not the opinion of the town, nor of the saintly Curate of Piansano, Don Giovanni Lucattini, who esteemed the two Religious Teachers very highly, calling them two very zealous teachers.

The ordinary school teacher of those days was not expected to be a learned person nor of much culture. The ability to read and write correctly, to teach Christian Doctrine and domestic science was all that was required, and Lucy's

Teachers knew all this to perfection. A pupil trained by these two Religious Teachers, Lucia Burlini, born on May 24, 1710 in Piansano, was placed in the local school conducted by the Lottieri sisters. The girl profited so much from the teaching of these two saintly souls and from the Christian atmosphere of the school that she attained a high degree of Christian perfection, receiving extraordinary mystical graces while under the spiritual direction of St. Paul of the Cross, who guided her soul for nearly forty years. She was buried in the Parish church of Piansano after she died on May 1, 1789. This had been the wish of St. Paul of the Cross who well knew that one day the Lord would single out the grave of Lucia Burlini. His prophecy was fulfilled and now steps are being taken for her glorification on earth.

In one of her spiritual conversations with St. Paul of the Cross, Lucia spoke of the *Maestre Pie* and of her deep gratitude for them.

"Yes, I know only too well," said St. Paul of the Cross, "the differences between those towns where the *Maestre Pie* have their schools and those in which they have none. In the former I always find faith and devotion, in the latter things are quite otherwise."

In his missions, St. Paul of the Cross never failed to exhort Catholic parents to take advantage of these schools and to have their children educated by the Religious Teachers.[1]

Good trees produce good fruits, according to our Blessed Lord. The seeds that produced good fruits in the soul of Lucia Burlini were planted in the school conducted by the two Religious Teachers. All the Christian Doctrine she knew was

[1] P. BERNARDINO. *Lucia Burlini.* Rome, 1952. Pag. 106.

A Fierce Storm Is Stilled by Lucy's Prayer

learned there and all the knowledge she possessed was acquired from the two teachers whom one priest and his Capuchin friend had called "ignorant."

Contradictions, persecutions, denunciations had been the lot of Christ's Apostles. Having taken up their apostolate, Lucy could hardly escape sharing their fate. Persecutions added new flames to her love of God and to her desire to save souls. She never stopped spending herself for Christ until that life itself was entirely spent in a perfect holocaust of service and love.

CHAPTER FOURTEEN

THE SPIRIT OF A SAINT.

"HUMILITY goeth before glory,"[1] says the Scripture. The glory of the Saints shows the splendor of their virtue; humility comes before virtue as foundations do before the superstructure of a building. True Christian virtue is based upon humility. As soon as pride drives humility out of a man's heart, sin enters, drives out all virtue, leaving only the sham of pharisaic justice, and so sin itself—of which pride is the beginning[2]—is even more hideous because of the false pretension of virtue. No wonder that St. Augustine regarded humility as a kind of synthesis of all moral doctrine: "Almost the whole of Christian teaching is humility."[3] Humility is not only necessary to virtue as its foundation but also for its protection: "Humility repulses Satan and preserves in us the gifts and graces of the Holy Spirit."[4]

Lucy Filippini's virtue was based on humility. Love of God and of neighbor gave the most characteristic and sublime expression to all her virtues. A saint is never found who was not

[1] Prov. 15:33.
[2] Ecclus. 10:15.
[3] *De Virginit.* 31.
[4] ST. F. DE SALES. *The Devout Life.* III, 4.

Lucy's Blessing Saves a Woman's Arm

humble, because saints know God well, and therefore know themselves better. Knowledge of self without knowing God begets pride and self-esteem. Knowing one's self in God is to know the truth about one's self and truth is the mother of humility. The Scriptures say that "where humility is, there also is wisdom."[5] There can be no wisdom, on the other hand, where there is no truth, and there is no truth where there is pride.

Knowing herself in God, Lucy understood that man is nothing in the sight of his Creator, because all he is has come from God. If sinful, man is worse than nothing before God. While the world praised and honored her, Lucy regarded herself as the last of all of God's creatures. "The wicked Lucy, the infamous Lucy"—this was the ordinary moral appraisal of herself.

During her staying in Rome, Lucy was honored by several ladies of the Roman aristocracy, among others Princess Altieri and her daughters who remained Lucy's most devoted friends for life. Lucy admired and loved the virtue in these noble ladies, not their rank, riches, and honors. A letter written by Lucy, less than two years before she died, dated July 5, 1730, says:

"I left Rome very mortified. Those married Princesses were adorned with such great virtue, and I myself—wearing the uniform of virtue—was deprived of all virtue! What will be my confusion on the Last Day! May God help me and grant me grace to amend my worthless life! . . . Please, do not forget the poor and useless servant of Your Excellency."

Lucy always sought that the low opinion she had of herself be entertained by others as well. Many were the ways and means she used to create such a lowly opinion and contempt for herself among others. When among strangers, she spoke of her miseries, faults, and shortcomings to them. Several times,

[5] Prov. 11:2.

during her stay in Rome, she walked through the city with her habit turned inside-out, asking for alms like a common beggar. With her Confessor's permission, she often mixed with the crowds of ragged and filthy beggars at the gate of monasteries in Rome to show the abject contempt she had of herself. This sense of humility was prompted in her by the love of the King of Heaven who dwelling among men had chosen a stable for His home and a manger for His bed. There was also the example of the Poor Little man of Assisi who had done similar things on visiting the Eternal City, and Lucy burned to share with him the chaste joy of sitting at the table of Lady Poverty, whose handmaid is humility.

Although Superior of her Religious Teachers, she regarded herself as their servant and always acted like one. Whenever she visited her school at Rome, she insisted even as General Superior of the Institute on humbly kissing the hand of the local superior. When in the company of her spiritual daughters, Lucy always took the last place among them. Even though far superior to her Teachers in intelligence and prudence, she humbly asked their advice whenever important decisions arose. Her humility however, did not prevent her from correcting faults and abuses in her subjects whenever necessary, yet even in exercising authority, Lucy found an opportunity to humble herself. After the correction had been made, she went down on her knees asking forgiveness if she had let her feelings get the better of her in reprimanding others. She did this not only with her spiritual daughters but also with the housemaid in case of a reprimand.

Judging from the deep absorption and the ecstatic look on her face during her long prayers, Lucy must have received many mystical favors and divine communications from God during those precious hours. If such was the case, however she never revealed anything to anyone except to her Confessor at his request. If other people asked her about the subject, she simply said: "All I do in my prayers is to ask God for mercy and forgiveness." She had no time and certainly no inclination to dwell on such gifts, much less to write at length about divine favors granted her in prayer. Like most of the great mystics, she carried within her soul the secret of the King to her grave. She lived on the highest plane of Christian mysticism, but wished the world to follow her example of humility. Her deep sense of humility shrank from anything that would involve a study of her gifts and merits.

In obedience to Cardinal Barbarigo, Lucy travelled by carriage or by litter when visiting the schools of the diocese twice a year. After the death of the Cardinal, however, she followed her heart's inclination and chose a little donkey for such travels, and even then, if the poor beast seemed to be tired, she would step down and walk for a long while. Her brother John Francis and her sister Elizabeth remonstrated with her on this point because they regarded such a means of transportation too undignified for a member of their family. The example of our Blessed Savior riding an ass, although he could have been carried on the wings of the Seraphim in splendor and glory, was too strong an incentive for her not to act as she did and to shun all worldly pomp and ostentation.

A scrupulous adherence to the precepts of evangelical poverty with all its discomforts and privations, austere penances and mortifications, even a bloody discipline several times a week, were the many expressions of th esame spirit of humility which pervaded every action of Lucy Filippini's life. Her diet was extremely poor and simple, her fasts frequent and prolonged.

Dry, stale bread, often covered with mildew, was all she took some days. When the administration of her schools was taken from her, and both her Institute and the schools were struggling for existence, as explained in the following chapter, her brother John Francis, who had settled down in Genoa and was very prosperous, went to see her often in Montefiascone, begging her to come live with him in comfort and peace of mind. She thanked him for his love and interest in her but she preferred her poor existence to all the riches and the comforts of the world.

This spirit stayed with her to the end, and she bequeathed it to her spiritual daughters in her Will:

"I, Lucy Filippini, knowing that I came into this world poor, naked, and miserable, wish to return into the hands of my God the same way I came. Therefore, I do bequeath everything that I have or possess to my sisters—the Religious Teachers— here present and now assisting at my passing away. I intend to place in their hands everything that pertains to my body, to my comfort, to my person, and even to my needs. I only beg them of one thing, to cover kindly my mortal remains with what is purely necessary and most humble. Of this I beg them for the love of Jesus."

Lucy's last will had been her constant will through life. As she dictated it, her spirit must have been contemplating two unforgettable scenes: the body of Christ carried to be buried in the tomb of a stranger, Joseph of Arimathea; the little brother Francis of Assisi dying on the floor of a poor narrow cell at Portiuncula.

The close relation between humility and charity has been beautifully stated by St. Augustine: "In the proportion we are cured of the swelling of pride, we are filled with charity. And

Lucy's Miraculous Communion

with what is he filled who is full of charity, if it be not with God?"[6] In no other creature was this relationship more manifest than in Her whom we call "Blessed among women." She esteemed herself a lowly handmaid of the Lord, full of humility, hence "full of grace," full of God: "the Lord is with thee." The Blessed Virgin Mary, whom Lucy loved and honored with singular devotion all her life, was the sublime ideal of the virginal purity, humility, and love of God she endeavored to imitate with her whole soul. In glowing terms she often gave expression to her hardent love of God: "O my God, I wish that such a flame of Divine love be kindled in my heart as to completely consume me, in order that You alone, my Lord, live in me and be my very life." A glow was often noticed suddenly on her otherwise pallid countenance, an index of the frequent impulses of the love of God, a flaring up of an inner flame that consumed her.

When news came that a new school was to be opened, Lucy's face became radiant with joy at the thought that more souls would thereby learn to serve and love God. Her every action was bejeweled with an act of perfect love of God when she made a good intention, repeating the act in the course of the same occupation. Even when talking with important people, she stopped the conversation for a few moments to recollect herself and to renew the good intention with an act of love.

Lucy slept very little at night, her soul conversing all the while with God praising, thanking and adoring Him. The Sisters who slept in the room next to hers heard often during the night her soft voice express the affection of her soul, singing some sacred hymn, like the following:

[6] *De Trinitate*, VIII, 8.

"Love Divine, come down to me! Fill my heart with thy sweet flame; from my soul, never part!"

Lucy's love of God was the dynamo that energized her apostolic work. The love of God, according to St. Gregory the Great, is never idle; it will do great things when it is authentic; should it refuse to work, it is not love but weak emotionalism. Since her youth Lucy had been a declared enemy of idleness, and she never tolerated it in any of her associates. The love of God, when authentic, manifests itself in works of charity, in the love of neighbor. "The love of God oftentimes not only commands the love of our neighbor, but itself produces this love and pours it into man's heart, as its resemblance and image."[7]

Lucy was only ten years old when out of charity she began to explain Christian Doctrine to children and to teach them how to pray. From that day the salvation of souls became her one great interest in life. There is no more divine act of charity than to cooperate with God in the salvation of souls. Lucy's schools, her missionary activity, her retreats, the care of the poor and the sick had one purpose, the salvation of souls. Her great works of charity prove that her love of God was genuine and heroic.

One very cold winter morning Lucy accompanied by one of her Teachers, named Lucretia Amari, had just entered the church in the town of Grotte di Castro when she noticed a famished little barefooted boy with only a few rags on, huddled unnoticed in a dark corner of the church. Deeply touched at what only her loving heart had noticed, Lucy could not keep from exclaiming: "Lucretia, is there no charity in this town? Quick, let's go home and get clothes for this little boy. It hurts

[7] ST. F. DE SALES. *Love of God.* X, 11.

me to see him shivering like that." They left the church at once; taking the poor little fellow by the hand, they went home and clothed him from head to foot and gave him food, telling him to come back whenever he needed anything. After her return to Montefiascone, Lucy often inquired about the little boy, asking: "Tell me, how is my little child getting along?"

A little girl in almost the same conditions of poverty and neglect went to Lucy one day asking for help. Herself without any means, at the moment, Lucy went to a priest to plead the cause of the poor child. She did it with such eloquence that she obtained all the money she needed to buy shoes and clothes for the child.

The sick and the poor became her special care in every town which she visited, helping them herself when she could, or interesting others in their behalf.

This maternal charity began at home; it was shown to her spiritual daughters whenever they suffered in body or in spirit or were in need of anything. She seemed to forget everything else when one of them was sick or afflicted in order to concentrate all her attention and care on that one person. "The charity shown me"—said one of her Teachers—"cannot be described. Twice she took me to Viterbo for medical consultation on a case of dysentry, which had troubled me for several months, accompanied by constant headaches. She paid no attention to expenses or discomfort in order to help me. On another occasion while traveling for my sake, she fell from the horse and broke her ribs." This particular Teacher thought that Lucy did all these things for her because of some special liking. "What do you think I do this for?" asked Lucy. "I do it as a sacred duty. What I am doing for you I would do for anyone else if I saw that she needed help as you do."

Miraculous Escape on the Bridge of Sutri

153

According to Di Simone, whenever Lucy visited the schools of the Institute she was to be informed by her Teachers about all their needs so she could provide for them. Not infrequently she deprived herself of the means of her own support to help her spiritual daughters. When informed that one of her Teachers was sick, no matter what the distance and the inclemency of the weather, she left immediately to take care of her and comfort her. No matter how serious their affliction, Lucy's spiritual daughters confessed that they never failed to be relieved through her motherly care and attention.

Almsgiving was another beautiful phase of her charity. "My daughters," she used to say, "give to the poor and do not deny alms to anybody, because it is charity that keeps our schools." When there was nothing else to give, Lucy would take objects and articles giving them to the poor to sell to relieve their necessity. She often received donations of money, food and materials of all sorts from her sister, Elizabeth. When Elizabeth occasionally visited her and found that all the things she had given had disappeared, she could not help wondering what had happened. "Ah, my dear sister," explained Lucy, "I have sent all your things to Paradise!"

In such acts of love of God and of neighbor, Lucy Filippini spent her life. By heroic charity and humility the Saint is recognized. Lucy Filippini had the spirit of a Saint, a spirit of charity and humility.

CHAPTER FIFTEEN

LUCY'S CALVARY.

THE tribulations of the Saints are many, but the Lord shall deliver them.[1] Very often deliverance is brought by the hand of the angel of death. Such was the case with the holy Martyrs of Christ. So it was to be with Lucy Filippini whose active but distressing existence here on earth ended after six years of a martyrdom of physical suffering and moral afflictions. The Lord delivered her from all her tribulations the day He called her to Himself from what had been truly in her case a valley of tears.

A tumor appeared on Lucy's chest during the year 1726, and its malignant nature soon became evident. With it came continuous fever and intense pain, more acute at night, making rest and sleep almost impossible.

Lucy had carried her crosses with indomitable courage ever since her childhood. With the appearance of this dreadful affliction she had reached her Calvary, the place for her final sacrifice, her crucifixion. The Savior of mankind had suffered not only the bodily torments of crucifixion but also the abandonment of his friends, the jeering and the wagging of heads, and the shrugging of shoulders of High Priests and Scribes who went to Calvary to insult him in his last moments, to accuse and

[1] Ps. 33:20.

155

discredit him before the world. Lucy was to follow her beloved Savior to the end, both in his physical suffering and abandonment and in his mental crucifixion, until Sister Bodily Death came to free her spirit from all tribulations.

In the year 1727, a year after the appearance of the cancerous tumor, the Bishop of Montefiascone, Pompilio Bonaventura, noticing perhaps that Lucy's dangerous sickness did not respond to treatments and might prove to be fatal, saw the necessity of giving a more permanent legal status to the schools of his diocese. As long as these had been under Lucy Filippini's direction and administration they had flourished and their number had increased even outside the territory of the diocese. What would happen to the schools without Lucy's leadership? She was now getting old and her painful sickness was curtailing her activity, presaging the end of her career. It would not be easy to find a successor to such an exceptional woman. The action of the Bishop under such circumstances was both wise and timely.

Cardinal Barbarigo, in his testament, had constituted Lucy Filippini's schools the sole heir to his estate, leaving the administration, however, in the hands of two high ranking dignitaries of the Cathedral Chapter of Canons. At the time of his death both the dignitaries were learned and saintly priests, Canon Luca Corneli and Canon Alexander Mazzinelli. These two priests, seeing the impossibility of taking care of eleven diocesan schools on the meager annual income of thirty dollars left the whole matter of administration to Lucy herself, knowing that she would do her utmost and keep the schools going. They were not disappointed in their expectation. Through great personal sacrifice, Lucy and her spiritual daughters managed not only to keep all the schools open but also provided a more permanent and reliable source of income for the schools by investing some two thousand dollars in real estate.

Careful and foresighted in her administration of the schools, Lucy had kept an accurate and separate account of the property acquired with Barbarigo's money and of that purchased with her own money—her own dowry, donations from her own relatives, personal benefactors, etc. The property acquired with her own money was registered In her own name, being thus separate from Barbarigo's estate. In the meantime it would remain a source of revenue for her schools and her Teachers, no matter what happened to the other estate under future administrators. The prudent foresight of this is obvious, and yet it was to be frustrated by the malice of men and a series of unfavorable circumstances.

Monsignor Sebastian Antonini held the office of Vicar General of the diocese of Montefiascone, for twenty-six years, from 1707 to 1733. Throughout such a long office, he exercised a powerful influence on the mind and the policy of his Ordinary, Bishop Bonaventura, becoming the sole arbiter of the problems of the diocese. Monsignor Antonini did not approve of the esteem and confidence shown by his Bishop to Lucy Filippini; much less did he approve of the money given her by the Bishop every year for the support of the schools. According to P. Bergamaschi, the Monsignor waited years for an opportunity to appropriate—with all the appearance of legality—whatever funds and property belonged to the diocesan schools, and to put the blame at that time on Lucy's "maladministration." The opportunity finally came with the death of Rev. Luca Corneli who died April 20, 1720. He had been one of the two dignitaries who had left Lucy Filippini to administer to the schools. The Vicar General was to recommend to the Bishop a successor to

Luca Corneli in the capacity of administrator of Barbarigo's estate. He recommended a close friend of his, Canon Anthony Falisci. Their plan was for Canon Falisci, in virtue of his new office and in obedience to Barbarigo's will, to request Lucy to give him back the administration of the school-funds. This done, he then accused Lucy of having unjustly acquired property for herself with Barbarigo's money and denounced her as fraudulent and dishonest.

Confirmation of such dark scheming and plotting against Lucy by the Vicar General, is found in a letter written by Lucy to Princess Altieri, dated September 3, 1731, after all the underhand plotting had finally been carried out, revealing the plotter's hand. In this letter Lucy, regardless of her great meekness and charity, calls the Vicar General *mio contrario*—my adversary. A contemporary witness, Canon P. Amari, of Valentano, wrote that Lucy, at this particular time, "was being persecuted and tormented by superiors and by friends . . . hated by many people of high position, publicly blamed for her spiritual exercises, defamed even in her reputation and her good name."[2]

On June 11, 1727, Lucy was summoned before the diocesan tribunal, the presiding judge being none other than Vicar General Antonini himself. Despite her intense pains and consuming fever, Lucy appeared before the tribunal of the Vicar General where she was requested to sign a statement, absolutely and completely renouncing all rights and claims to any property she had acquired herself for the benefit of the schools, at the same time binding herself never to have recourse or make complaint to higher authorities on these matters. The above statement contained substantially the idea of the Bishop, but a captious

[2] F. DI SIMONE. *Lucia Filippini.* Pag. 93.

form was prepared by the Vicar General with the purpose of ensnaring the unsuspecting Maestra Santa. In obedience to her Bishop, Lucy signed the official statement, renouncing even her personal dowry which had been invested in the property she had purchased. The Bishop's decree contained two practical clauses, one referring to the superintendent or superior of the schools, another to the administrator of the school-funds. According to the decree, the Superior of the schools was nominated by the Bishop, after hearing the opinion of the two ranking dignitaries of his Cathedral Chapter; and "because said office of Superior had been laudably held by the Signora Lucia," she was confirmed in office.

The other clause made provisions for the appointment of an administrator of all the funds and the revenues for the support of the schools. On December 27 of that year, the Vicar General proposed as administrator Canon Angelo Processi, who was more than willing to cooperate with him. With the excuse that he had to carry two separate accounts in the administration of the schools, he asked that Lucy hand over to him all documents pertaining to the administration of the school-funds, together with all the money and property on hand. Lucy obeyed, but in so doing she was left without any documentary evidence to defend her own conduct against future charges in the administration of the schools. In the meantime her enemies could not be checked as to the abuses of their administration.

The nefarious work of exploitation started immediately. The condition of the schools was at the time prosperous. Lucy had eight hundred gold dollars on hand, plus some wheat and a quantity of barley. She was forced to hand over the cash and all of the wheat and barley to the new administrator. When several bills became due, at the end of the month, Lucy went to the

Vicar General asking for funds to meet the obligations. She received nothing. Extreme poverty and privation of the most elementary things in life became the rule in all the schools and the Teachers' Convents. Under Lucy's administration neither the schools nor the Teachers had ever lacked anything; now under the new administration everything was lacking.

Poor Lucy who at this time was ascending her Calvary with the cross of a fatal and painful sickness on her shoulders, needed by doctor's order to go to Viterbo several times for whatever treatments were known in those days. She did not have a penny left for her own cure. The saintly Canon Mazzinelli, scandalized at the outrageous conduct of the new administration, interceded with the Vicar General and the new administrator in favor of Lucy. They granted "three dollars and fifty cents in order that the Signora Lucia may use this sum in going to and returning from Viterbo for the cure of her indisposition." Under such adverse circumstances Lucy's health could hardly improve. Her mental suffering was even greater than her physical pain.

About this time, the news of Rose Venerini's death added more gloom to the darkness gathering around Lucy's Calvary. Rose Venerini was called to her reward in Rome, on May 7, 1728, and was buried in the great Jesuit church in Rome—Il Gesù—near the chapel of St. Ignatius Loyola. Lucy cried and prayed for her dear friend and associate, feeling that very soon she herself would follow her. She was now the only survivor of that generation of great souls. She felt more alone than ever in this world because she saw men whose duty should have been to assist and help her and her work now bent upon destroying them.

While offering to God all her pains and humiliations for the preservation of her schools, Lucy did not fail to use such human means as prudence and justice demanded. During the summer of 1730, she went to see her influential friend and benefactress, the Princess Altieri, at her summer palace in Oriolo, begging her to call the attention of the higher authorities in Rome to the distressed situation of her schools in the diocese of Montefiascone. In consequence of this appeal, the Pope's Almoner— Lucy's superior—went to Montefiascone to examine the situation towards the end of October of that year. He comforted and encouraged Lucy and her Teachers, at the same time he suggested that Lucy prepare a memorandum on the whole matter to send to the Holy See, adding that he on his side would not fail to help her. Lucy did as requested and commissioned a legal expert to prepare the memorandum. Unfortunately for her, the expert omitted some necessary items and facts and the omission caused the failure of the memorandum and new recriminations against Lucy.

The Holy See, as is customary, sent the memorandum to Bishop Bonaventura for explanation. In reading it the Bishop was surprised to see that Lucy was practically asking for the abrogation of one of his official acts—the decree concerning the administration of the schools—and that no mention was made of all the money he had personally contributed every year for the support of the schools. He, therefore, left Montefiascone for his winter quarters in Tarquinia, asking his Vicar General, Monsignor Antonini, to study the memorandum and to send a complete explanation of the facts to the Holy See. The Vicar General waited for no better opportunity than this. In his reply to Rome he clearly emphasized all the facts omitted in the memorandum attributing the omission to malice and deceit, and covered up all the wrongs of the new administrators, leaving Lucy and her Teachers to take the blame for the present situation of the schools. From this time on the work of exploitation continued with impunity. During the year 1731, the last year of Lucy's life, the schools of Montefiascone received no support whatever from the new administrators. The Religious Teachers carried on, on the meager offerings of pious persons. Because of the discrepancy between the two reports, the Holy See could not take any decision but waited for further information.

In the meanwhile, Lucy's time on earth was running out, but in the midst of all these afflictions, her spirit remained calm and serene, full of faith in Divine Providence. In a letter written to Princess Altieri, on January 20, 1731, she remarked: "The whole matter still remains in the dark. The blackness of my sins must be the reason; but since this is the Lord's own business, He will take care of it. We, on our side, will do all we can, because the mercy of God will not fail those who trust in Him. Perhaps He wants to see me humbled first and then everything will be fine."

Indeed, Lucy was the grain of wheat that had to die and be buried first before it could bring forth fruit: "Unless the grain of wheat falling into the ground die, itself remaineth alone. But if it die, it bringeth forth much fruit."[3] She had to die while waiting in vain for a settlement of the painful problem, seeing her lifework threatened with ruin, with no recognition for all her sacrifices. It began to look like a big failure. Yes, it was the seeming failure of Calvary, a necessary prelude to the glory and the triumph of resurrection.

[3] John, 12:24.

CHAPTER SIXTEEN

THE BRIDEGROOM COMETH.

IN the darkest of the night a cry was heard: "Behold the bridegroom cometh."[1] It was a very long, dark night before the virgin soul of Lucy Filippini heard that cry from a messenger of joy, the Angel of Death. Her immortal spirit, rising above all human miseries and the wreckage of her earthly home, in the purest and most rapturous joy trimming her lamp went forth to meet the Bridegroom, the burning flame of her zeal and the shining light of her virtue unquenched by death's icy breath.

While persecutions and humiliations continued, during those last eventful years of her life the pain and the anguish of her dreadful sickness increased steadily. Nothing, however, ever prevented Lucy from attending with her customary zeal and devotion to her great mission of love. She continued her classes for girls, the meditations for the women of the town, her works of charity, and the visitation of her schools. At times she was so completely exhausted at the end of the various exercises that many thought she would succumb any moment to the violence of her agonizing pains and she had to be put to bed.

A religious priest, who at this time had asked Lucy for prayers for the success of his mission, received the following reply from her:

"Poor Lucy is sick and she has to stay in bed most of the time. She herself needs to be recommended to God, nevertheless, she with her companions will do as you request. Pray that the

Lord may hear us, for we on our side shall not fail to ask him to give you a tongue of fire as He gave to His Apostles when they received the Holy Spirit."

Completely resigned to the will of God, wishing with the Apostle "to be absent rather from the body and to be present with the Lord," nevertheless, in obedience to her Confessor and to please her spiritual daughters, Lucy accepted all the medical care offered her.

During the year 1729, Archbishop Albini, Almoner of Pope Benedict XIII, and Lucy's Superior, invited her to come to Rome where she could find better medical care and treatment than in the small town of Montefiascone. Lucy thought it was a duty for her to accept the gracious invitation of her Ecclesiastical Superior and was ready to go. As she was preparing for her trip she received a letter from one of her Directors, a priest of the Society of the *Pii Operai*, who in order to try her spirit came out with a censure of her conduct in accepting the invitation of the Pope's Almoner, saying that she seemed to be too much concerned about her bodily health and was trying to rid herself of a cross which the Lord had sent her for her own profit.

Having read this letter, Lucy changed her mind about going to Rome and decided to decline the offer made by the Almoner. In her reply to her Director, Lucy wrote:

"As far as I understand from your most welcome letter, Your Reverence does not approve of my going to Rome for my cure. I am more than willing to heed your most noble sentiments in this matter. Indeed, our Jesus suffered all the time in this world, I, on the contrary, am too selfish in trying to avoid suffering. I keep telling people that in this world we have no other good than that of suffering for the love of God, then, I myself try to avoid the cross. What a fool am I! Ask our Lord to grant me a little of His love, then I, too, will be able to imitate those generous souls who find no consolation except in suffering. I certainly can prattle, can't I? Woe to me, who have never associated good deeds with all my good words!"

The Director who had given the advice became alarmed when he learned of the gravity of Lucy's sickness from other people and hastened to tell Lucy to accept the Almoner's invitation to go to Rome for her cure, because this was the maniwest will of God.

Thus Lucy went to Rome—her last visit to the Eternal City. While there she underwent a series of painful treatments, but all in vain. Seeing the uselessness of all human remedies Lucy decided to return to Montefiascone where her presence was demanded by the serious difficulties of her schools. Like a brave soldier who though mortally wounded rises again with a supreme effort from the blood-stained ground to face the onslaught, so Lucy with her life ebbing away returned to the field of action to defend and protect her schools and her Institute to her last breath.

About four months before she died, Lucy wrote a letter to Princess Altieri, dated November 29, 1731, in which she pleaded for the protection of her schools. A careful reading of this letter shows that all earthly interests seemed to fade away at the thought of eternal life, of going home to God, which was uppermost in her mind in those days.

"It is quite sometime now since I have heard from my good Princess. I beg you to let me know how you are, because I am a little worried, remembering that you were not quite well when I left [Rome]. I am not so well myself. I do not know what the Lord has in mind for this miserable creature. Please, Excellency, ask God to forgive me, and having forgiven me, to take me whenever He pleases, because it will be so much better with Him, Who is all our Good and outside of Him there is no other Good. If Christians had the true light of God, they—like our Blessed Lady—would look at death with longing and at the present life with sorrow. But because we are so blind, we love this miserable life more than the true life which is full of bliss. How foolish of me not to be pining with desire of that Supreme Good, which is the true, the permanent, and alone deserving to be named Good. A little more love for this transcendent Good! Pray much for me, for your prayers can help me a great deal."

Lucy's affection for all the members of the Altieri family is expressed in many tender words in which the thought of Heaven returns again and again. She knew that this was the last letter to her great friend and benefactress. Her last greetings clearly reveal her mind; it was her parting farewell:

"Good-by, my dear Princess! My most humble regards to the kind Prince. Tell him that I recommend my poor schools to his care. Whether living or dead I recommend this work to him."

The day after this letter was written, Lucy suffered a fainting spell while at school. When she recovered consciousness she refused to be taken to bed before giving the meditation to the ladies who were already gathered there. After the meditation she felt so weak and so tormented with pain that she had to lie down and stay in bed.

Her cancerous tumor had broken out causing a dreadful sore, causing excessive hyperaesthesia and contraction of all her nerves so that she became completely paralyzed. She lived in this painful and paralyzed condition for the remaining four months of her life. Her tongue alone was unaffected by the general paralysis and she made use of it in praising, thanking, and blessing the Lord. This fact caused the attending doctor to admire her for he well knew what excruciating pains she suffered. It was the same with other people who assisted her. When convulsive pains befell her, no other words came from Lucy's mouth but these: "I thank you, O Lord!—Lord, have mercy on me!"

At other times Lucy was heard praising God with song. She often invited her companions to help her in thanking God for having allowed her to suffer a little for His sake. Calling her Teachers around her bed of pain she asked them to join her in singing the *Te Deum* and the canticle *Benedicite*. Those who came to see her could not help exclaiming: "Where do you find your strength to bear so much pain?" "In the grace of God," was Lucy's answer. Then, resuming her prayer, she added: "Lord, forgive me! Lord, I thank you! Lord, have mercy on me! Jesus and Mary, draw me up to you!" With these last words she obviously alluded to her present state of helplessness and her great desire to go to Heaven. Many were moved to tears to hear Lucy pray in this manner on her bed of pain.

Lucy who had carried her cross to Calvary was now nailed to that cross. Her crucifixion lasted from the last day of November to the twenty-fifth of the following March. During these months the people of Montefiascone showed their great love and esteem for the *Maestra Santa* who had brought untold blessings to their town. When the serious nature of her sickness became known, constant prayers went up to heaven for her recovery from both the clergy and the laity. By order of the Bishop, all the priests of the diocese said the oration *Pro Infirma* daily at all Masses for Lucy's recovery. The thousands of women and young girls who more than others had received the fruits of Lucy's apostolic work vied with one another in asking God to spare the Saintly Teacher. Lucy's associates and spiritual daughters could not bear the thought of losing their mother at such a critical time for the Institute, and they multiplied their prayers and their penances hoping that God would hear them. But Lucy's course was about over and the Lord had decided to give her the crown of glory for a life well spent in His service.

It has been observed that a dying person's last thoughts are usually for the mother, so were Lucy's. She had known really only one mother in life, her heavenly Mother. Whenever a Feast of the Blessed Virgin Mary came near during those four long months of her crucifixion, Lucy inquired from her doctor whether she could hope to die on that Feast of the Madonna.

Springtime had brought violets, hyacinths, and all the flowers of spring to the verdant shores of Lake Bolsena, and the first swallow had been seen in Montefiascone. On March 19, 1732, Lucy called in one of her spiritual daughters and with a radiant expression, like one who is announcing joyful tidings, said to her:

"The Angel who announced to Mary the Incarnation of the Word will be also the messenger of my death," meaning that she would die on the coming Feast of the Annunciation.

That same day—the Feast of St. Joseph—Lucy received the last Sacraments of the Church with profound reverence and devotion. Soon after the sacred rite, she was seized with a new attack of paralysis which, this time, affected even her tongue, and her voice was stilled forever. Consciousness remained for awhile, for when asked by the Priest whether she wished to receive the final Absolution for the dying with Plenary Indulgence, she gave signs of assent. After she had received the Absolution, she fell into a coma. In this state of unconsciousness, with no struggle whatever, she lived till the morning of March 25, the Feast of the Annunciation. She seemed to sleep peacefully during that long night of nearly six days.

Towards noon of March 25, a messenger of God must have cried out to her: "Behold the Bridegroom cometh!"[1] Lucy awoke suddenly from her long sleep, opened her eyes fixing them towards heaven, and smiled at some celestial vision. That smile remained on her face, but her eyes soon closed, never to open again.

Thus a burning and shining light was taken out of this world, that morning of March 25, 1732, when Lucy Filippini's wonderful soul went home to God. The afterglow of that light still endures and it will remain forever in the firmament of the Church, because "those who instruct many to justice shall shine as stars for all eternity."

In the liturgy of the Mass the Church often sums up the whole life story of her Saints in one or two symbolical expressions. This is how it synthesizes St. Lucy Filippini's life and work in the Mass said in her honor on her Feast, May 11:

"It is good for me to cling to my God, to put my hope in the Lord God: that I may declare all Thy praises, in the gates of the daughter of Sion."

"O God, who so wonderfully didst raise up Blessed Lucia, Thy virgin, for the promotion of Christian piety among the people, and through her, for the education of youth, didst gather a new family within Thy Church, grant that by following her precepts and examples we may attain unto the rewards of everlasting life."

[1] Matt. 25:6.

SOURCES

ANDREUCCI, Andrea, G., S.J. Vita della serva di Dio Rosa Venerini. Rome, 1868. (First edition, Rome, 1732).

BERGAMASCHI, Pietro. Vita della Venerabile Lucia Filippini. 2 Volumes. Montefiascone, 1916.

————, Le Origini delle Maestre Pie. Rome, 1926.

CELI, S. J. Le Origini delle Maestre Pie—*Civiltà Cattolica,* from Jan. 3, 1925, to Feb. 20, 1926.

DI SIMONE, Francesco. Vita della Serva di Dio Lucia Filippini. Rome, 1868. (First published in Rome, 1732, the year of St. Lucy Filippini's death).

MARANGONI, Giovanni. Vita del Servo di Dio Card. Marco Antonio Barbarigo. Montefiascone, 1930. (This is the first publication of a manuscript of the early eighteenth century, once attributed to Luca Corneli, now more commonly to Marangoni).

MAZZINELLI, Alessandro. Istruzione per Regolamento delle Scuole della Dottrina Cristiana delle Zitelle. Rome, 1868.

REGOLE del Pontificio Istituto delle Maestre Pie Filippini. Vatican City, 1951.

SALOTTI, Card. Carlo. La Santa Lucia Filippini. Rome, 1930.

SUMMARIUM Processus Faliscodunensis Beatificationis et Canonizationis Servae Dei Luciae Filippini—Documenta—Litterae Postulatoriae—Animadversiones.

VARIA Documenta Pontificia: ex Actis Clementis XIII, Leonis XII, et Leonis XIII.